LECTURES

ON THE

SYMBOLIC CHARACTER

OF THE

SACRED SCRIPTURES.

BY

REV. ABIEL SILVER,

MINISTER OF THE NEW JERUSALEM CHURCH IN NEW YORK.

"The words that I speak unto you they are Spirit and they are Life."

"Without a Parable spake He not unto them."

NEW YORK.

D. APPLETON AND COMPANY,

443 & 445 BROADWAY.

1863.

PREFACE.

THESE Lectures were not written with a view to their being printed, but were designed as simple and plain lessons of instruction to those not acquainted with the symbolisms of the Word. And they are now permitted to go to the press only at the solicitation of many who have heard them.

They were delivered during the past winter, in the city of New York, to audiences in which there were many strangers, and no two congregations were alike. This made it necessary to refer frequently to the relation which exists between spiritual things and natural things, alluding often to *First Principles* and their effects, and thus keeping the Law of Analogy continually before the mind.

I am now asked to give them to the public, as they were delivered, under the suggestion that the repetitions they contain, will be no more than minds, unacquainted with the Science of Correspondences, may need to enable them to easily understand them. And I accede to the request, assuring the reader, whoever he may be, who has not looked into the spiritual sense of the Holy Word, that if he has a desire to do so, and will study the Science of Correspondences, and read these simple illustrations of the Sacred Scriptures, with a sincere desire to become acquainted with the Word of God, that he may the better know his heavenly Father, his own soul, and the true way of life, that he may walk in it, the Lord will open to his mind a new field of thought, and lead him to a Fountain of heavenly Wisdom which he will prize more valuable than all things else; for he will find therein the true life of heaven. That he may do so is the prayer of

THE AUTHOR.

NEW YORK, *April,* 1863.

CONTENTS.

CHAPTER XV.

PAGE

CHAPTER XVI.

CHAPTER I.

REASONS WHY THE LITERAL SENSE OF THE WORD OF GOD MUST SYMBOLIZE A HIGHER SENSE.

"The words that I speak unto you, they are spirit and they are life." (John vi. 63.)

WE are now commencing a course of lectures upon the symbolic character of the Sacred Scriptures, or of the Divine Language. But, are we truly sensible of what we are undertaking? Are we, indeed, conscious that the language we purpose to explain is infinite, that God's words must contain infinite ideas, and that, to fully comprehend them, would require the wisdom of the great Jehovah—a capacity so far beyond the reach of men or angels? All this we fully believe. And we also believe, that we can learn to appreciate the meaning and force of God's language, only in degrees according to our states; and that we can do this properly, only as we become acquainted with God's nature and character. For if we would enter into the real life and spirit or any book, we must know the qualities and character of the author; for the real author lives in his words and his works. And, as from the language of men, we are introduced to a knowledge of their minds ; so, from the language of God, we may become somewhat acquainted with the will and wisdom of our heavenly Father. For God lives in his language. The words which He speaks, "They are spirit and they are life." And that spirit and life are God Himself in His wisdom and love.

But what is the divine language? In its broadest sense it is everything that manifests the Lord's qualities. He is the author of everything; he lives in everything, and speaks in everything, either directly or indirectly. But His speech is understood according to the state and ability of the reader. Some see it in the light of divine wisdom, and understand it aright to the extent of their capacity. Others see it in the light of their own self-derived intelligence, and understand it not as it really is, but only as it appears to them to be.

But it is of the nature and character of God's revealed Word, rather than of the book of Nature, that we are to speak this evening ; and more particularly, of the reasons why that Revelation must possess a symbolic or spiritual sense distinct from the literal sense. But in doing this, and in all our lectures, we shall aim, not so much at the profundity and depth of the divine Wisdom and Word, as at its simplicity and plainness. For everything perfect and divine is in itself deep and obscure ; far deeper than finite minds can fathom. Human wisdom can never reach the starting point, so as to comprehend the full cause of anything ; for Infinity is involved in that. Our efforts, therefore, in these lectures, will be to simplify and bring the real, spiritual things out from their secret enfoldings, into the plain daylight of the reasoning faculties of man's natural mind; where he can see them in the light of science, take hold of them with the arm of his judgment, turn them over and about, and look at them on all sides, in the relation they bear to one another, to man and to their Creator.

Now the first and perfectly conclusive reason, why the Holy Word contains a spiritual sense within the literal, is seen in the law of analogy, which pervades the entire Word, and which shows the relation between spiritual and natural things; between the world of mind and the world of matter; between God and nature; between the mind of man and the universe of things. But this argument has no weight with a person, who is not acquainted with this law of analogy, or science of correspondences. This argument, therefore, we cannot use in this evening's discourse, as our lectures are designed for persons unacquainted with that science. But it will gradually present itself as the truth and beauty of that science are seen and understood, as the law is applied to the illustrations of the Word, as we proceed with these lectures. For the science of correspondences is the great rational test of the divinity of the Sacred Scriptures. By means of it are clearly understood the history of the Creation, the Garden of Eden, the Fall, the Flood, the Prophecy of Ezekiel, the Second Coming of the Lord, the Descent of the New Jerusalem, and the wonderful things declared in the Apocalypse. Upon the truth of this science, as an infallible key to the otherwise hidden beauty and glory of the divine Word, the receivers of the doctrines of the New Church are ever ready to rest the entire question of their new religious faith.

Does any one disbelieve or doubt, that the Lord, as the "Word," which was in the beginning with God and was God, and which was manifest in the flesh, is now actually making his second coming in the spiritual or internal sense of the Word, for the establishment of a new religious order of things, which will eventually bring all to see eye to eye, do away with all sin and contention among men, and really make all things new ?—I say, does any one disbelieve or doubt this ?—Let him test the ground of his unbelief by the truth or falsehood of the science of correspondences. We court this test of all who candidly desire to understand the Holy Word. For, of the result of such an investigation, we have not the least doubt. We ourselves (with thousands of others) have weighed the ground of our own former unbelief in the same balance, and found it wanting. And all, who have ever sincerely examined into the merits of this science, have come to the same conclusions, and alike understood the doctrines of the sacred Word. The reason of their agreement is, that correspondences are a *real science*. For, as the science of geometry, by the light of natural truth, brings every close investigator of its principles to the same results in the solution of its problems ; so, also, does the science of correspondences by a higher, and yet, equally philosophical light, bring all its true and faithful investigators to the same conclusions as to the doctrines of the Word. For all truths are eternal verities.

They are ever and unchangeably the same. About them, when seen, men do not differ. It is about falsehoods, and where truths are not seen, that the intellectual world is contending.

The doctrines of the Word, when seen in the light of correspondences, become themselves the indisputable evidence of their own truth. This is the reason why the students of this science agree in divine things. And it is the very reason why the watchmen, at the second coming of the Lord, are to "see eye to eye."

The science of correspondences is a language. It may be denominated THE language. For it is the sure language of Jehovah. It is therefore a living language. It is the only language that has spirit and life. It is a universal language: the language in which not only the Holy Word speaks, but the mountains and streams, the winds and the ocean; yea, earth and skies and universal nature with her ten thousand tongues are speaking to us. Does any one doubt the existence of such a language? Let him learn to read it. No one who has ever learned it has any such doubts. Does he say no one ever has learned it? How does he know that? Thousands of persons, entitled to respect, say they have studied it, and find it to be a most sure and certain language. Where, then, rests the weight of evidence? Who is the best judge of a book, he that has read it, or he that has not?

By this science, the Sacred Scripture is convincingly proved to be the Word of the Infinite Jehovah. All its parts thereby blend into harmony. The darkest and most obscure passages are opened and explained;

and the simplest portions are filled with profound wisdom. Every passage is, indeed, seen to be "Profitable for doctrine, for reproof, for correction, for instruction in righteousness" (2 Timothy iii. 16), according to the apostle's declaration. But without this science, has any one found it to be so? If the Bible was given by God to man to teach him something, was it not intended to be understood? Has God endowed man with reason, addressed him as a reasonable being, said to him, "Come now, and let us reason together" (Isaiah i. 18), given him His Word as a rule of life, to show him what he must do and what he must not, and, at the same time, interspersed throughout the Word thousands of things which he can never understand, and which are of no use to him? Not so. Infinite Wisdom has not so indefinitely expressed Himself that He cannot be understood

The difficulty is with man. He, by a false and evil life, has lost the pure language of analogy in which God speaks. But, by the divine mercy of the Lord, that language is again restored. That sublime key to the inexhaustible treasury of intellectual wealth contained in the Word and Works of God is now mercifully made known. The great seminary of scientific wisdom has become accessible to man. For this divine key not only unlocks God's book of Revelation, but also, at the same time, His book of Nature. And as we are thereby conducted within the veil of the letter of the Word, and permitted to feast upon the pure bread and water of life, and to admire the glory and beauty of that divine sanctuary; so we have, also, a passport within the veil of universal nature, where we find, enthroned, pure spiritual philosophy, expounding the invisible ligaments which unite heaven and earth; elucidating those otherwise incomprehensible affinities which exist between life and matter, God and nature, the mind and the brain, the soul and the body. In passing this veil, we enter the School of all schools, look up to the Teacher of all teachers, and study the Science of all sciences. The books we read are the Books of all books — the book of Nature and the book of Revelation. They are books published by the same Author, they illustrate the same principles, and lead to the same conclusions. Both books are necessary to the proper study of either. All the objects in nature, are so many indices, pointing to the history of their creation, and the cause of their existence; and refer us for information to the written Word, to which they are the grand concordance. At such a seminary, with such books, and such a Teacher, we may obtain heavenly wisdom and feast on angels' food.

But, to a mind unimbued with the science of correspondences, what we have said are mere assertions rather than reasons. Let us, then, assign some reasons why the Holy Word has a spiritual sense within the letter. And, first, it is because it contains divine thoughts and feelings, which are infinite in wisdom and love. Now, the literal sense is in man's language. The meaning of the words of that language is limited. Men understand their full import. There must, therefore, be a sense within and above the literal definitions of the terms, or it is the language of men only, and not of God. And the Lord Himself declares that there is such a sense, when He says to us, "The words that I speak unto you, they are spirit, and they are life." For He made this declaration to teach men, that He does not mean by the words 'flesh and blood,' what they are defined to mean in man's language; but that He means infinitely more. For spirit and life are infinite and eternal things; such things as He desires to feed our souls with, that they may live for ever. Now, if we know that 'flesh' is a symbol of goodness, and 'blood' a symbol of truth, we have, at once, a definite though limited understanding of what the Lord there means, and it is highly interesting and instructive. But, otherwise, we cannot distinctly understand what He does mean, by eating His flesh, and drinking His blood. And the correspondences here are exceedingly beautiful. Our physical man is composed, principally, of flesh and blood: our spiritual man, if in order, is composed of goods and truths. Thus; there is a perfect correspondence between the mind and the body. Now, it is because the natural substances, of which the body is composed, correspond to the spiritual substances of which the mind is composed, that the mind and body can be united and exist together.

Again, all spiritual life is by means of the union of goodness and truth; and all physical life, by means of the union of flesh and blood. Therefore, if we well understand the science of correspondences, we may know, from the fact that, as the drawing of the blood from the flesh produces physical death; so, also, the separation of goodness and truth in the mind produces spiritual death. We must love the truth, or die spiritually. And so the natural things which we eat and drink to supply flesh and blood to the physical man and keep it alive, have their perfect correspondences in the goods and truths which the Lord says the mind must eat and drink, or have no life in it. Thus, with this scientific light, the mind is illuminated, the soul cheered, and the heart refreshed ; but without it, that beautiful Scripture is involved in clouds of uncertainty, and its richest blessings are unenjoyed. And when we further know, that evils and falsities are goods and truths perverted, and that such substances, when taken into the mind, poison the affections and thoughts, and make the soul diseased, we may also know that the poisonous substances of the earth, to which those evils and falsities correspond, will, when taken into the body, make it also sick and diseased. 'Flesh and blood,' therefore, when mentioned in the Word, may mean, either things good and true, or things evil and false, according to the sense in which they are used. With this scientific light in the mind, the true use of the words 'flesh and blood,' wherever expressed, throughout the entire Word, may be readily seen ; and thus, Scripture, otherwise dark and obscure, will emit a clear and certain light.

Now, there is much said, in the Word, of 'blood,' and of 'innocent blood ;' of 'shedding *innocent blood;*' of 'taking away *innocent blood;*' of 'condemning *innocent blood;*' of 'putting away the guilt of *innocent blood;*' of 'betraying *innocent blood;*' of 'sinning against *innocent blood.*' And yet, there can be no such thing as innocence, or guilt, in material blood. This, everybody must know. All understand that it is the mind that is innocent, and not the blood. Blood is therefore used because it denotes a living principle of the mind. And it is only because truth filled with love is the very life of an innocent mind, and blood, as the life of the body corresponds to that life, that the blood of such a person is said to be innocent. It is declared in Isaiah that, "The sword of the Lord is filled with blood"—an expression which strikes terror to many minds ; and yet, its real meaning is beautiful and consoling. The *sword of the Lord* always signifies the divine truth of the Word, in its powers to conquer and destroy evils and falsities. Therefore a sword is said to go out of the mouth of the Lord, because he speaks the truth. "The sword of the adversary," mentioned in the Word, signifies falsehood. For the Devil is "A liar, and the father of it." Then the phrase, "The sword of the Lord is filled with blood," would read, by correspondence, "The truth of the Word is filled with life." *Sword* denoting truth, and *blood* life.

Another reason why the Word must contain a spiritual sense is, because, without it, that Word seems, in many places, to directly contradict itself, and cannot be reconciled, but by the spiritual sense. But in the light of the spiritual sense, all is made rational and clear, beautiful and instructive. For example, the Lord commands us, saying, "Thou shalt not kill ;" and yet, he says again, "Cursed be he that keepeth back his sword from blood." (Jer. xlviii. 10.) Both passages are full, open, and unqualified ; and are applicable to every man. Without the spiritual sense they cannot be reconciled. But by the science of correspondences, we see that, besides the death of the natural body, there are two kinds of death, two kinds of life, and two kinds of killing, treated of in the Word. There is the life of the love of good, and the life of the love of evil : one is heavenly life, and the other is hellish life. If we die unto the love of good, we become alive unto the love of evil : this was the fall of man. And so, if we die unto the love of evil, we become alive unto the love of good : this is regeneration. Therefore, the Lord says, "He that findeth his life shall lose it : and he that loseth his life for my sake shall find it." (Matt. x. 39.) That is, he that findeth his spiritual life, shall lose his selfish life : and he that loseth his selfish life for the Lord's sake, shall find his true spiritual life. Then, if we remember that blood, which is the life of the body, and corresponds to the life of the soul, may, when mentioned in the Word, denote either hellish life or heavenly life, according to the sense in which it is used, we shall at once, see the truth and the harmony of the two contradictory passages mentioned above. In the first—"Thou shalt not kill," we are commanded not only not to kill the body, but also, not to destroy any principle of goodness or truth in the soul : in the second, "Cursed be he that keepeth back the sword from blood," we are taught, that, unless we conquer our evils—unless we shed the blood of our carnal life—our love of self, by the sword of the spirit—the divine truth—we shall be lost, or be curse

Again, we read in the gospel of Matthew, "They that take the sword, shall perish with the sword," and also, the Lord says, "He that hath no sword, let him sell his garment and buy one." (Luke xxii. 36.) Now, this, in the letter alone, is strange teaching. Who can know what it means? We answer, No one, without the spiritual sense. Who can see why the Lord should command us to sell our garment and buy a sword, to perish with? Men may say it is figurative language. And they will interpret the figures differently, according to their several tastes. But they must rest in uncertainty, till they see the spiritual sense. Then, they will have no doubt of its meaning. For that sense is definite and sure, reasonable and clear. "They that take the sword shall perish with the sword," therefore, means, that, They that take the *sword of the adversary*, or falsity, and use it, will, by continuing their false-witnessing, destroy everything truthful and good in their souls; and thus they will perish with the sword. While, on the other hand, he that has not commenced the regenerate life, who has no true sword of the spirit, must sell his garment of self-righteousness, must put away his filthy rags of covetousness and sin, and buy the sword of truth. Garments, which are the clothing of the body, denote the outermost deportment, or clothing of the mind. And the outermost things of the sinful mind, are its most external, selfish, and worldly thoughts and actions. These must be put away before we can fully possess the sword of the spirit in our heart.

Again in Isaiah, the Lord declares of His church

that "They shall beat their swords into plow-shares, and their spears into pruning-hooks; nation shall not lift up sword against nation, neither shall they learn war any more." But soon after, in Joel, He says, "Prepare war; beat your plow-shares into swords, and your pruning-hooks into spears, and let the weak say, I am strong." Now, God's Word is universal, reaching to all men. These commands are as applicable to us as they were to the Israelites and the Gentiles. How shall we obey them? They command us, in the letter, to do two diametrically opposite things. And a command to do one thing forbids us to do the opposite. In the covenant to love our neighbor, we are bound not to hate him. The command, not to lie, includes the behest to tell the truth. We must therefore look beyond the letter to find what God would here teach us. But from what we have already said of the sword, it may readily be seen, that the swords and spears which we are to beat into plow-shares, and pruning-hooks, must be the swords and spears of the adversary, or false principles. But what are the plow-shares and pruning-hooks which we are to have in their stead? The plow-shares must be those divine truths which will penetrate deep into the heart, and bring on a thorough repentance, and thereby plow, or, as it is called in the Word, "Break up the fallow-ground of the heart," that the seeds of truth may be sown in an humble and contrite soil. And the pruning-hooks are those watchful and corrective truths of the Word with which we may notice, and cut off the dead and unfruitful branches from the tree of our life. But what, then, are the plow-shares and pruning-hooks which we are commanded to beat into swords and spears? They are, of course, the very opposites of the others. The plow-shares are those false and contentious principles, which plow, or stir up the selfish feelings or soil of the natural heart, engendering strife and ill-will, and thus, preparing the ground to receive new and fresh seeds of falsehood and selfishness. And the pruning-hooks are those principles, opposed to truth and virtue, which are always ready to prune from the tree of spiritual experience, every good shoot it may send forth. The false plow-shares and pruning-hooks of the mind, must be converted into swords of truth, and spears of wisdom, wherewith we may fight against the headstrong evils of humanity and subdue them.

Again, David prays that the Lord will scatter all those that delight in war; and yet he also says, "Blessed be the LORD my strength, who teacheth my hands to war, and my fingers to fight." (Ps. cxliv. 1.) These literal contradictions contain within them, spiritual harmonies, which the science of correspondences only can reveal. By that science we see that David desires that the Lord would scatter all the wicked spirits and evil principles that delight to war against things good and true, and that he blessed the Lord for teaching him, by the truth, how to fight against those evil influences. In all David's prayers to the Lord to destroy his enemies, he never means persons, but the evils which are in them and in himself. There is not a syllable in all the Psalms, when their true light is seen, that contradicts that beautiful precept of our

Lord which says, "Love your enemies, bless them which curse you." But this love has relation to the persons, and not to their evil principles. Evil principles with their falsities are the only things to be hated. Against them our faces should be firmly set, wherever they are.

Again, we are expressly commanded in the Word to Honor our father and mother ; and yet the Lord as expressly says, that if we do not hate them we cannot be His disciples. Now, without the spiritual sense, these statements are perfectly inexplicable ; no light has ever been thrown upon them, or evolved from them ; nor can there be any without the science of correspondences. We must see that the Bible, in its most essential meaning, treats of mental and spiritual things, and that pure, virtuous minds, or such principles of the mind, must have the divine Love and Wisdom for their Father and Mother. God, in the unity of his love and wisdom begets them ; and therefore, they are called *children of God:* while on the other hand, corrupt and depraved minds, or such principles of the mind, must have evil and falsity for their father and mother. The Devil, or the love of evil and falsity in the complex, in the union of their ill-will and deceptiveness, begets or perverts them ; and therefore they are called *children of the Devil.* Thus heavenly Love and Wisdom are the Father and Mother we must honor ; and hellish evil and falsity are the father and mother we must hate and forsake ; while our own natural parents, and all human beings, we must love and try to do them good.

Again, the joyous song of the angels at the birth of

our Lord was, "On earth peace, good will toward men;" and yet, the Lord says, "Think not that I am come to send peace on the earth: I came not to send peace, but a sword." In the spiritual light, these angels and the Lord are both seen to be in harmony. The Lord is indeed the Prince of Peace; and yet He is a God of war and of vengeance. But his warfares and vengeance are not against men, but against their evils. Thus He comes to send the *sword of truth* that we may have peace through victory over our evils. For without the truth we can never know peace.

Again, it is written in the Holy Word that, "It repented the Lord that He had made man on the earth, and" that "it grieved Him at His heart." It is also written, that "God is not a man that He should lie, nor the son of man that He should repent." Now, how could Infinite Wisdom, Goodness and Perfection grieve? How could He who knew all things from the beginning, and does all things right, do anything to repent of? How could Infinity and Immutability—He who is the same yesterday, to-day, and forever—how could He repent? His ways are not as our ways, nor are His thoughts as our thoughts. It is an apparent truth that God repents and grieves; those emotions can be felt only by man; and when mentioned in reference to God they mean His mercy. The very essence of true repentance and grief are mercy and compassion. These heavenly emotions belong to the Lord.

In order to bring the letter of the Word down to the states of wicked men, God is often represented as being not what He really is, but rather, what He appears to them to be. For this purpose He is represented as possessing the depraved passions of men; is said to be angry, wrathful and revengeful. And it is often asked by persons who begin to see that those qualities cannot belong to a Being who is *Love*, why the Word was so written. And we answer, It was for the wisest and best of purposes. It was so written that it might be capable of teaching poor, natural, fallen, wrathful, revengeful man the way of life and salvation. To teach another we must come to his state, to the sphere of his understanding, to his language and mode of expression. Now, an angry man will believe those angry with him, who oppose him. He who will get angry at his children for disobeying him, or seek persecution and revenge upon those he thinks his enemies, would suppose that his God would do the same: and he would think it right that God should be angry and punish his enemies. This man, God comes to, in his Holy Word, according to his state. He warns him to "Flee from the wrath to come," and threatens him with damnation in hell. At the same time He kindly tells him how to avoid these evils. He commands him not to steal, covet, and so forth. Now, the natural, wicked man knows it is wrong to steal, or deceive. He would punish any one that would steal from him. And in seasons of mourning, sickness, or other afflictions, he hears the Holy Word preached, and his own character comes up before him in a light which makes him shudder. He is afraid of the wrath to come, because he feels guilty and thinks he deserves it, and in a spirit of repentance, he begins to amend his life and plead for mercy. Here, "The fear of the Lord is the beginning of wisdom." But as he progresses, he gets the love of God which casteth out fear, and he now finds that God was not angry, but loved him all the while; that it was *his own opposition to God* which made it appear as though God were opposed to him, and which is the reason why the Word was so written.

The words which the Lord speaks, they are spirit and they are life. But, for the natural man to see and understand anything of that spiritual life, they must be brought down into man's common words, as vessels or symbols through which they can be apprehended by analogy. And though those words have a literal meaning, and may give a correct literal history of events in this world, yet they also teach, by correspondences, a spiritual history of things in the world of mind. The human words are so selected and arranged by divine wisdom as to contain this spiritual sense. And in many instances, the literal events mentioned are only appearances, not realities, and are given for the sake of the spiritual sense.

We should bear in mind, that we are in a world of appearances, that the *real* world is out of sight; that in this world we, to a great extent, speak according to appearances. If we did not so speak, we could not be understood by the generality of mankind. We speak of *looking through miles of space*, and of *beholding the mountains and the spread-out landscape;* and so it appears; while the reality is, that the image of the landscape is brought by the light, and pictured upon the retina of the eye. We have looked through no space. We see not beyond the skin of our eyes. So, we speak of *hearing the thunder from the clouds;* but the drum of the ear makes the noise. We speak of *the blue arch of heaven, the vaulted skies, the revolving stars,* and *the setting sun :* but there is no arch there ; the stars are stationary bodies ; and the sun does not set. We talk of *the colors of objects;* but the colors are from the varied positions of the rays of light. Things have no color. And the Holy Word speaks of such things, according to appearances, because men's states require it.

Now to come to the reality of even these natural things we must have science. What do we know of nature without science ? And yet, God's Word comes to us, clothed in the habiliments of nature. It treats of invisible things. It teaches the nature and character of the Invisible God, of our own invisible being, and of the laws of the invisible world ; so that " The invisible things of God, from the creation of the world are clearly seen, being understood by the things that are made, even His eternal power and Godhead." But the Word cannot possibly teach this without science. The invisible things of God cannot be seen through the things that are made without the science of correspondences, any more than we can understand the planetary systems without the science of astronomy. For, as we cannot understand the deceptive appearances in God's book of Nature without the deductions of natural science, so, neither can we understand the apparent discrepancies and contradictions in God's book of Revelation without the spiritual science of correspondences. And all who rightly study the Word by that science, alike receive the true doctrines of the Word, with as much certainty and harmony of sentiment, as they can the problems of Euclid, or any other scientific deductions.

We have endeavored, in this discourse, to advance some reasons why the Word of God must have a spiritual sense, and to show that dark and contradictory passages can thereby be reconciled and made plain. The age has now come, when the free inquiring mind demands a *reason* for what it is required to believe. And such irreconcilable contradictions, as those we have cited, are causing many religiously disposed minds to begin to hesitate, and doubt the divine origin of the Bible. And thus, insinuating skepticism steals in upon their hearts step by step, till the blessed Word loses, to them, its divine sanctity and power. What a consoling and joyous thought then, that there is now an opportunity for such a mind, to become rationally convinced that there are no contradictions in the blessed volume, that all its parts are harmonious and consistent, that there is a glory and beauty beaming through the letter of every page and sentence, at the sight of which the scoffer becomes dumb, and the sincere skeptic opens his mouth in humble praise and adoration of the blessed Jesus, and hugs the Holy Word to his bosom as heaven's best gift, and man's unfailing treasure! "Whoso is wise and will observe these things, even they shall understand the loving kindness of the Lord."

CHAPTER II.

THE ORIGIN OF LANGUAGE AND THE LAW OF THE DIVINE SYMBOLS.

"There is no speech nor language where their voice is not heard." (Ps. xix. 3.)

WE are now to take a general glance at the nature, origin, and use of language, and of the law of analogy, or language of correspondences. What then is language? It is any mode of expressing or conveying ideas; whether by words, looks, actions, signs, symbols, fables, metaphors, parables, representatives, or correspondences. Whence is language? In its outward speech it is all from nature. From the things of the universe, and the life which is in them all, speech originates. "There is no speech nor language where their voice is not heard. Their line is gone out through all the earth, and their words to the end of the world."

Let us then take a glance at Nature; see what she is, how she speaks, and what she says. Now, there are two worlds, a spiritual world and a natural world. The spiritual world is the world of mind, and the natural world is the world of matter. Mental things are composed of spiritual substance, and material things of natural substance. The world of mind is the world of causes, and the world of matter is the world of effects. And as there can be no effect without its cause; so there can be nothing in the world of matter which has not its proper correspondent in the world of mind; nor can there be anything in nature, which does not point for its origin to the spiritual world.

What then do we mean by the science of correspondences? What is it? It is the law of analogy which shows the relation between these two worlds. Correspondence is not a metaphor of speech, nor a trope in language, but a universal law of creation and providence. A metaphor, or simile is the mere resemblance which one natural thing may be thought to bear towards another, or towards a spiritual thing. Correspondences are the actual, effective relation which exists between spiritual and natural things. It is a higher law than can exist between matter and matter, or spirit and spirit on the same plane. It is the union of inner things with outer; or higher things with lower, and is the great law by which both the spiritual and natural worlds subsist from the Lord. For as an effect cannot exist without a cause, so neither can a cause without an effect. Now, God is the great *efficient* cause of all things. Therefore, every created thing, whether human, animal, vegetable, or mineral, bears a correspondential relation, either directly or indirectly, to some one of the infinite varieties of the divine principles. For the entire universe is an out-birth from God. It is not God. But it is the effect of God. God is the cause, and He fills the universe with life. And it is because the effect is related to the cause that He can fill it with life. This relation is the law of analogy, and is the means of constantly holding the universe in existence. Suspend this law for one moment, and universal nonentity is the consequence.

Now, the great end and object of the Creator in giving existence to the universe was, the production of His own image and likeness in created intelligences whom He could for ever bless and make happy by His own goodness and truth, whereby they could know Him, and love Him, and thus be filled with heavenly bliss. But how can we know that God's object and effort in producing the universe was to bring forth His own image and likeness ? We can know it, because that law obtains throughout the whole universe of things. Everything that has life is in effort to produce its kind. God has imparted that law of His own nature to all created things. And the effort of all nature to carry out that law, emphatically bespeaks that principle in God.

Now man, in true order, is in the general image and likeness of God. Any other created thing in true order is only an image of some principle or principles in God or in man.

The order of the outward creation of the world was, from lower things to higher ; first minerals, then vegetables, then animals, and finally man : thus orderly and gradually approximating by higher and purer organizations the real divine image, until God finally crowned the creation with man, as the sum total and embodiment of all things below him. When all but man was created, and everything was in readiness to produce man, the vast variety of things scattered all over, and throughout the universe, were but humanity in fragments : every single thing was an image of some principle which was to be in man ; and it took them all, combined, to make up the full man. Man could not exist until these things were created ; for upon them his body must subsist ; and through them his mind is to be educated. And when all these materials were brought harmoniously together, in man, and all was pronounced good, the vast universe corresponded to man, and man to his Maker.

Who cannot see that the things which God creates, must be, in their degree, like Him, so far as a finite thing can be like an infinite ? His love desires their creation, His wisdom devises the mode, and His power executes it. And they come forth, not out of nothing, but from Himself ; and He is the very life of their existence. The withdrawal of His love from any created object, would at that instant destroy it. It takes the same power to sustain which it does to create. Preservation is perpetual creation.

Thus we see, that during the whole process of creation, God was making man. God is the Infinite MAN. And all things that he makes must be expressions of Himself as they come from His hands. But He can make nothing infinite. He cannot add to Himself. Infinity is all : everything is involved in it. The creation of lower things is only a finite expression of qualities in the Divine Being.

The highest individual image of God is the wisest and best man, or angel. But even that image is constantly being improved by the reception of further goods and truths for its ever-expanding mind and increasing wants. And the affectionate union of various wise and good minds into a society, imparting to each other what the Lord gives them, is a higher, and more full image than that of an individual. And this image will be forever improving by the constant advancement of each of its individuals, and by the continual accumulation of more individuals. For no two men are alike. Their various forms and qualities indicate the variety of the divine principles. Every addition, therefore, to the Grand Man, supplies a deficiency in the general image, and makes it more full. But the perfection of the original never can be reached : because Infinity never can exhaust Itself by giving forth new expressions of its parts, and filling them with life. The reason is, the Fountain is Infinite, and the human beings given off, or created from it, are only various finite expressions from it.

But, to return to the period when in the process of the creation all things were in readiness for the production of man ; when the vast variety of human principles lay scattered throughout the mineral, the vegetable and the animal kingdoms, in living, speaking forms ; when all nature was a beautiful page of mental symbols in physical robes, without an admirer on earth ; with no created rational being to read the expressive characters of that wonderful book, and to love and worship the Author ; then it is that we behold Man, making his appearance—Man, the sum total of the creation, the connecting link between God above him and nature below him, and thus, the crowning act of the creation.

And as man was made above all other things in the scale of creation, by being endowed with rationality and freedom, and at the same time embracing within himself all the various qualities of life which animated the natural world, therefore, life had thereafter to be supplied to nature through the medium of man. For life ever flows from God, through higher things into lower.

But we have said that correspondence is the relation which an effect bears to a cause ; and it may be asked how the lower orders of creation could correspond to man, and yet be the first created. The reason is this : the principles which constitute a true man, always existed in God. He is the infinite Man, and man is His finite image. In the etérnal purposes of God, therefore, man, in potency, and indeed every human being, always existed ; not as distinct created individuals, in self-consciousness ; but yet, in the divine mind, perfectly distinct and objective ; for God is the infinite Man : and one of the fundamental laws of the spiritual world is the ultimation of internal qualities in objective forms. By this law there always went forth from Jehovah, and was manifest before Him, in substantial human form, His own image. This image was not Himself, but the outgoings of Himself for further ultimation in the actual creation of man. And, in bringing man down into nature as the created image of God, the lower orders of creation were the ultimated effects of those outgoing principles of humanity which constitute man. While, therefore, in point of time, the lower orders of things were first, yet, in spiritual reality, man, in the full image of his Maker, was first, in the divine mind, in outward, substantial, objective form, though not in actual individual creation. And that substantial form was the medium cause, in the power of God through which the various principles of man's nature became ultimated in the world, and clothed with matter.

Man, therefore, is the medium of conjunction and communication between the natural and the spiritual worlds, being in one, as to his soul, and in the other, as to his body. And, being the medium of life from God to lower things, he imparts his qualities to the divine stream, as it flows through him. Consequently, as man fell, the various things below man partook of his depravity, became changed and modified according to the various vicissitudes and changes of man's states and qualities. Thus, nature became corrupted through man's vileness. The earth brought forth thorns and thistles ; the wild beasts became quarrelsome and ferocious ; serpents and reptiles, became poisonous and troublesome ; and hawks and owls, moles and bats, annoyed the human race.

Still, the world corresponded to man ; and sad, though faithful, was the tale it told of his conduct and vileness. The book of Nature still spoke to man with her ten thousand tongues, but how changed were many of her accents ! To the people of the primeval age, before the fall, all her tones were sweet and harmonious ; she spoke the sure Word of the living God. Therein they read the history of their creation, the character and laws of God, and the nature and quality of themselves. There was no truth which men needed to know that this book of nature did not teach or indicate. It was, to them, a medium of infinite wisdom. Upon what page soever their eyes rested, they saw, as by intuition, the true nature and character of the scene in its living aspect. So clearly did they look through nature up to nature's God, that the very names which they gave to the various objects of the creation indicated and expressed the peculiar quality and character of those objects. This book of nature was written in the pure language of analogy. They could read it in that language. It was a universal language, understood and read by all alike : for it spoke from life through qualities clearly indicated by their forms and uses. And it is now, as then, in itself a universal language ; and all who truly see it understand it alike.

But the people of that golden age read not this language in the light of their own wisdom ; nor did they have to learn it, as we do, by the light of the Word through the study of the law of analogy. They had never sinned, they were the open and willing recipients of wisdom from their heavenly Father ; and, in that state, they could not mistake His teachings through nature, nor the language in which He spoke : for it was divine language, unchangeable and universal. It is the only language used in the spiritual world ; and in the full millennial day it will be universal again upon the earth, as it was before the fall. It is alike the language of nature and of Revelation.

The Holy Word, if correctly translated into all the various languages of the earth, would still have the one universal language of analogy pervading the whole work; and in that light it would be read and understood alike by all. The various languages of men would be lost in the glory and beauty of the one divine speech.

The reason why men, before the fall, saw the language of analogy by intuition is, because their wills and understandings were in harmony with the divine love and wisdom, and acted with them. Men had then but a mere shade of will and thought of their own. They had a self-hood, and were free; and it appeared to them as though they saw and felt from their own knowledge and desire. They had not learned to exercise that self-hood against the divine order. Therefore they saw and enjoyed the divine light as though it were their own. And, for a long time, the language of correspondences was the only language of the earth.

It was the first written language. When men first began to put their thoughts upon the barks and leaves of the trees, and the skins of beasts, they did it in the hieroglyphics of nature. They had no other language. Pictures of the objects in nature instead of the living originals became the expressive symbols of men's ideas. And there was no thought, feeling, passion, or propensity of the mind, which this language could not delineate to the life, and much more correctly than any other language could do it; because man's spiritual qualities had given the very forms to the objects in nature which would be selected to represent those qualities in man. The written language therefore, could not possibly be mistaken by any one who understood the science of correspondences, even at the present day. Did the people of that age wish to express, upon parchment, any attribute or character of their Creator ; in the book of nature they saw Him in living lines, and any expression of His character could be delineated therefrom. Then, in very act and deed, "The invisible things of God, from the creation of the world, were clearly seen, being understood by the things that were made ; even His eternal power and Godhead." And did they wish to correspond with their friends at a distance, or narrate a history of events, this mode of writing was amply sufficient.

But, in the process of inventions, the period arrived when a new language from the use of sounds expressed by means of letters and words was invented and introduced into use. But even in this language men still conveyed their ideas, as before, by natural symbols : for though they did not paint any longer the objects of nature, yet they spelled and used the names of those objects, and therefore continued to look by correspondences, through the objects themselves for the quality of the ideas. For example : — they had been accustomed to paint the lamb for innocence, the serpent for subtlety, the hand for power, the eye for the understanding, the heart for the will, the ear for obedience, the stars for knowledges, the moon for faith, the sun for love and sometimes for the Lord ; and so on. But now they used the names of these things, which conveyed the same ideas. For the names of things always indicate their qualities. Indeed when these things received their names such names, were given to them as signified, by analogy, their quality. So that the change in the mode of writing, did not change in the least, the character of the language. It was still the language of correspondences—the language of God. And the names of the natural things, just mentioned, now signify in the Word what is stated.

This is the true original language. And in this language of correspondences, Moses, a man skilled in all the wisdom of the Egyptians, wrote the Pentateuch, in the Hebrew language, a language peculiar for the expression of the qualities of things by their names. In no other language than that of correspondences could the Bible possibly contain the Word of God; for no other language can have, in itself, "Spirit and life."

But as man, by sinful habits, became less and less spiritually-minded, and gradually sank into sensuality and naturalism, so this sublime language lost its beauty and glory, until its gold became as dross and passed away; but not without leaving its expressive memorandums upon the pyramids of Egypt; in the records of the Druids, in Oriental literature, in the fabulous stories of antiquity, in the idolatrous worship of the Gentiles, in Heathen Mythology, in German superstitions, in the poetry of all ages, and, even, faintly, in the present profane languages of the earth.

But, from all these remains the spirit and life have departed; and the consequence of the loss of this science is, "Confusion of tongues" all over the earth.

Men cannot now, certainly understand each other. Their words have no definite meaning. They quarrel from the want of a sure way of expressing their ideas. The hottest mental combats often end in the perception of the fact, that the parties both meant the same thing; but misunderstood each other's words. Now, there can be no other sure and certain language than that of analogy. It is *the* language, because God's language. The confusion of tongues, at the building of the tower of Babel, was from the loss of this language; for that confusion was spiritual. It was a confusion of thoughts as well as of words. Although that history appears short, yet it embraces a long period of time, during which men forsook the Lord's language or words of truth, and the true way of life, and undertook to build up a tower of their own self-hood, which could give them heaven in the light of their self-derived intelligence. And by this course, they finally lost the science of correspondences, and the true meaning of God's words. And then, as a matter of course, they misunderstood each other. They had no standard to go by. They contended among themselves about the truth of the Word, and consequently divided into parties and factions, and scattered abroad. And hence, the innumerable variety of languages, and of religious sects and conflicting creeds; and even of divers opinions among individuals of the same sect, upon the meaning of God's Word.

It is therefore from false, and not from true views of the Word, that men are divided. Truths are eternal verities. They are ever and unchangeably the same.

And all truths are in harmony, and sustain each other. About them, when seen, men cannot differ. It is about falsities, altogether, that the Christian world is contending. Falsities are all dark, unstable, deceptive, and mysterious; fit grounds for contention and strife, and for the proud display of self-wisdom; and constant changes of opinion are and must be taking place among those who build upon such grounds: while those who build on the "Rock of ages"—the spiritual truth of the Word rationally seen in the light of analogy, never can change their views, nor disagree in their doctrines, unless by sin they lose their language. When this light is seen in the study of the Holy Word, it will as inevitably lead all sincere students of divinity to the same conclusions in every jot and tittle of the Word, so far as it is seen, as the light leads to the sun from which it flows. The reason is, the investigation is carried on by a scientific law, and that law is divine. The reason, therefore, why men who read the Word in the science of correspondences, differ not in its doctrines, is the very reason why men differ not in mathematics; it is because, in both instances, the truths are indisputable. If, as we believe, there are no two persons who, without the light of this science, agree as to the doctrines of the Word, and no two, who have it, that disagree, the question, as to its truth, becomes a startling one.

Now we wish it distinctly nnderstood, that this language or science was once universal; that it has been lost, and is now revealed; that the revelation has been made by the Lord himself in fulfilment of prophecy, and not by any man; that "The Lion of the tribe of Judah . . . hath prevailed to open the book, and to loose the seven seals thereof," and has evolved this science from nature and the Holy Word, and not from the mind of any man; and has caused its general elements and rules to be recorded in the works entitled the ARCANA CELESTIA, the APOCALYPSE REVEALED, and the APOCALYPSE EXPLAINED; and that when we read these works, and learn this science, and behold its light, we obtain both the science and the light from the Holy Word, and from nature, and not from those works except as the light shines in them from the Word.

As we read those wonderful books with an humble and teachable disposition the Holy Word comes up constantly before us with newly shining pages, which grow brighter and brighter as we progress, until the heavenly harmony and beauty of the Word become so absorbing to the mind that we lose all sight of the writings we are reading, and the Word itself becomes its own interpreter—its own revealer of the divine law in which it is written. One passage throws its light upon another, and receives back the other's lustre in blending beauty, and their united blaze is responded to by a third, and all these are embraced by a fourth, and so on, till every sacred text we see becomes an evidence of the truth of all the rest, and the whole blessed Word, so far as we behold it, stands before us in symmetrical glory and beauty, a perfect whole, in an infinitude of parts, all in harmony. And though we are lost in the depth and immensity of its wisdom, yet, we are lost in light and not in darkness. And every advance we make in the regenerate life enables us to drink still deeper at this inexhaustible fountain of the water of life.

Now, are there any persons present who are unacquainted with this science? let me affectionately invite you to turn aside and see this great sight, how the bush burns and is not consumed. Would you have a view of the light of the sun of righteousness, as it shines from the interior of the Word, removing every obscurity from the letter, and reconciling all apparent contradictions? come and take a scientific view of the divine language. Does infidelity at times trouble you with doubts, and would you see those doubts flee before the light of the Gospel like the fogs of the morning before the rising sun? would you see the Holy Word in a light which will prove to you, beyond the possibility of a doubt, that it is the Word of the great Jehovah? look at it in the light of correspondences. It is not a foreign light, brought to the Holy Word to enable us to see its teachings. It is its own scientific light, beaming from its own pages. Would you be able to close the mouth of the skeptic by truths irresistible, when he scoffs at the serpent's tempting Eve and talking with her; or at the woman's being made of the rib; or asks you how long the seventh day was on which the infinite God rested; or who was Cain's wife, and where he found her? stop not at the surface of the word, but look within. Would you see the ladder which Jacob saw extending from earth to heaven, and would you hold communion with God thereon? you may find it in the Holy Word; it is the relation between cause and effect; it is that sublime way which leads through nature up to nature's God. Would you see the wonderful vesture of our Lord, woven without seam from the top throughout? you must see the spiritual sense of the Word in its perfect harmony and oneness; while the letter, or outward garments, are parted among so many sects. Would you see the burning bush unconsumed? you must see the literal sense of the Word shining with inward fire, or brilliant with spiritual truths from the love of God. Would you, like Moses, turn aside to see this great sight, how the bush burns and is not consumed? Come not to gratify idle curiosity, come with an humble and teachable disposition, desirous to know what God says to you, that you may obey Him; for like that venerable lawgiver, you may spiritually hear God call unto you "Out of the midst of the bush," saying, "Draw not nigh hither: put off thy shoes from off thy feet, for the place whereon thou standest is holy ground." (Ex. iii. 4, 5.) The shoes, which are the clothing for the feet, denote the lowest and most outward things of the mind—our carnal proprium. This must be put off before we can truly appreciate the internal sublimity and beauty of the Word.

The spiritual sense is the *sanctum sanctorum* of the Word, where we may hold communion with Him who is "Of purer eyes than to behold iniquity." We may see something of the natural philosophy of this sense by the science of correspondences while we are in a natural and selfish state of mind; but, to feel it in our hearts, and see its inner glories, we should approach it with a suitable sense of the great distance between our own state and the purity of its teachings. We should come then, with humility and meekness, praying to the Lord that He will open our understandings, that we may behold the wonderful things written in the Law. And, if we have truly sincere desires, a lively faith and ardent hope, and look into the Law of analogy with elevated understandings, rationally opened to receive instruction in a reasonable way, we shall behold, and understand the wonder which St. John saw—"A woman clothed with the sun, and the moon under her feet, and upon her head a crown of twelve stars:" or, in other words, we shall see "The holy city, New Jerusalem, coming down from God out of heaven, prepared as a bride adorned for her husband:" or, in still other words, The church of God, with its doctrines shining in spiritual light; for the Lord God and the Lamb are the light thereof.

Doubting not that this New Church is the very thing now needed and designed to prevent the universal reign of skepticism, to restore reverence for the Holy Word, to open, elevate and enlighten the human mind, that it may overcome and put away the love of self and the world which now so universally reign, and become filled with the love of God and the neighbor, and be happy; I appeal to you, as you value order, light, love, peace, purity, and heaven, to examine these things. O, turn not away from this call; for it is a call to a true "Feast of reason and flow of soul." We call you to no instantaneous reception, in a way you will not know how, of something you will not know what. We invite you to look at nothing unreasonable, and to believe nothing you cannot understand. Come, then, to the Fountain of Wisdom, and drink the truth into your souls understandingly. Come willingly, come cheerfully. come inquiringly. "The Spirit and the bride say, Come. And let him that heareth say, Come. And let him that is athirst come. And whosoever will, let him take the water of life freely," (Rev. xxii. 17.)

CHAPTER III.

THE ANALOGY BETWEEN THE UNIVERSE AND THE MIND.

"For then will I turn to the people a pure language, that they may all call upon the name of the LORD, to serve Him with one consent." (Zeph. iii. 9.)

WE are to glance this evening at the Scripture analogy between the material universe and the human mind. This analogy is strikingly manifest, everywhere in the Holy Word, by the science of correspondences—the sure language of God—in which that Word is written, and which, according to the prophecy of our text, the Lord promises to make known to the people. This promise is now being fulfilled. The Lord is now turning to the people a pure language, that they may all call upon the name of the Lord, and serve Him with one consent. There was a time when there was but one language upon the earth. The Lord declares in the 11th chapter of Genesis that, "The whole earth was of one language, and of one speech." And again He says, in the same chapter, "Behold, the people is one, and they have all one language."

Now, it is certain that that language has been lost.

The people are not all of one speech now. Nor are the people of any one language all of one speech, in that language. Indeed there are no two persons of any one language, that understand that language alike. The reason is, the language itself has no stability nor sure definiteness. This is because it has lost its roots. True, the language we use purports to take root in many others. But these languages themselves, and even those of them which are called dead, or fixed languages, have, to men, lost their roots. Nature is the ground in which all true language takes root. And the law of analogy is the only light in which that root can be truly seen. We know the dead languages are not fluctuating and changing like those in common use. But the reason is, they are not used. It is to the conservative nature of the Hebrew and Greek languages, that we are indebted for so correct a knowledge of the Holy Word as we now have. And it is therefore of the divine Providence that they became dead, that they could better preserve the Word. Those languages still take root in nature. But men, by the loss of the science of correspondences, see not where, nor how that root exists. Hence the uncertainty which hangs over the precise meaning of many things in even those languages; and particularly in the Holy Word, where many things are written solely for the sake of the spiritual sense, and therefore where no shadow of a rational meaning can be seen without the law of analogy.

But the Lord says, prophetically, in our text, pointing to this age of the world, "Then will I turn to the people a pure language, that they may all call upon the name of the Lord, to serve Him with one consent." Now what can this pure language be, in which all the people will call upon the name of the Lord, to serve Him with one consent, unless it be a language which will give them all the same ideas of God and of His Word? and also, unless it be that very language which the people had, when the whole earth was of one speech, and all called on the name of the Lord? And who that sees the science of correspondences, and reads the Word by it, can doubt that the time has now come, in which that prophecy is being fulfilled, when he sees persons of every nation and kindred and tongue and people embracing this language, reading the Holy Word by it, understanding it alike, and beholding therein the Lord Jesus Christ, as the one Lord, whom they can all serve with one consent? And what other language can the Lord turn to the people than the one they have before had, and which He gave them? He says He will turn to the people a *pure language*. What is a pure language? It is certainly something above human, like its Divine Author it must be divine, definite, and sure—the same yesterday, to-day, and forever. Such is the language of analogy; and such is no other language.

Let us then continue our investigations into the nature, origin, and use of that language; that we may see the relation between the physical universe and the human mind. The ancient Greeks called man a *microcosm*, or little world. They considered him an epitome of the *macrocosm*, or the great world or visible system. This was from correspondence; and although this word microcosm—this comprehensive and graphic exvression of human nature has, for a long time, been considered fabulous, and has become nearly obsolete, though still retained in English dictionaries ; yet it is, at this day, rising from obscurity, replete with meaning, and speaking with light and life. And many are now investigating, with admiration and delight, the countless volumes of mental philosophy contained in this one word *microcosm*, it being expressive of the embodiment of all the elements of the universe in man, as the connecting link between God and nature.

Man, then, being a microcosm ; what is there, what can there be, in God's Word or His works, that does not treat of man, and also of God, the infinite man, the great eternal prototype of all created things ? This view of the subject furnishes us, at once, with the reason why God, in giving us His Word to teach the way of life, has written that Word in the symbols of nature ; for that language, like its Author, has a divine character ; its essence is the life of the universe, ever flowing from God, and well might He say, "The words that I speak unto you, they are spirit, and they are life." God's language, therefore, is as much superior to man's language as His works are superior to man's works, or, as He Himself is superior to man. His language, could we read it all, would teach us all things ; for everything that God does speaks ; and a single sentence, or even word of His, contains an infinite variety of things. It is a part of everything. Thus, it is infinite in its essence, in its qualities and in its relations. And by the relation which every part of the Holy Word bears to all the other parts, the whole and all its parts may be proved to be true; for every part has God in it in His wisdom and love, and therefore we may learn from it forever; for God is perfect in the least things as well as in the greatest. And though our minds are lost in its unfathomable depths, and insurmountable heights; yet, to our consolation and joy, we are lost in light and not in darkness; for we are in the midst of an infinity of truths, each corroborating and confirming the truth of all the rest, so far as they enter into the mind; so that there are no contradictions. But still, the willing receiver is not so lost as not to be able constantly to ascend higher and higher up the holy mountain, beholding, as he rises, newer and brighter glories in Wisdom's light.

Does this look like exaggeration, or fancy-sketching? Who, we would ask, will, at this day, presume to fix limits to the extent to which man may advance in wisdom and knowledge? Being made a recipient of God's wisdom and love, and having the Lord for his teacher, where shall he stop? Why may he not yet know how the trees grow, and the plants bloom, and see and understand the causes which are operating behind the curtain of matter?

Now, as man is a microcosm, having within him all the living elements of the macrocosm; and as God, the infinite man, is the Author and Father of all, is related to all, and is giving existence and life to all; so, therefore, the history of man is the history of everything; a knowledge of man is a knowledge of everything; and the study of man is the study of everything. And God's Holy Word embraces that whole vast history. It is an entire history of man—past, present, and prophetic: a history of his origin, nature, and destiny; of what he has been, is, and will be, embracing all time and eternity. And in coming to that Holy Word for light, our investigations will be much facilitated by bearing in mind, that the internal sense from the beginning to the end of the volume, treats expressly and entirely of the nature and character of God, of the various creations and falls of man, and of the consequences, to man, of his being either good or evil, true or false. This is the one, and entire history.

By the various creations, and falls, and re-creations of man, embracing all his diversified qualities, of every shade and character, which are described throughout the Word, are meant, the establishment, consummation and succession of churches of every grade; or the regeneration of man in all the minutiæ of the process. This is the one constant theme of the Sacred Word. And what else could it treat of when that theme embraces everything? for whether we say the Bible is a history of the church, or the history of man, it is the same thing; for the church in man is what constitutes him man. This is what gives him the image and likeness of his God. This is because the essentials of the church are love and wisdom in man, from God, going forth into action. Whatever, therefore, may be the apparent subject of the letter of the Word, we must look, by analogy, through what appears on the surface to matters of the mind—to things human.

Where the creation of natural things is mentioned, the internal sense treats of the creation of the spiritual things to which the natural things correspond. And as all things in nature correspond to principles in the mind of man, therefore, a history of man's spiritual creation or regeneration could be perfectly described by a history of the creation of natural things, whether those natural things were created in the order mentioned to describe the spiritual creation or not. Thus, in the very commencement of the Holy Word, the spiritual creation or regeneration of man, the microcosm, is described by a parabolic history of the creation of the universe, or macrocosm. And this creation of natural things is narrated in such order, by the divine wisdom, as to teach, by correspondences, the precise process of the regeneration of man; or of the growth of a human mind from spiritual infancy, up into the image and likeness of God, in every particular of the proceedings; so that men, in the light of the spiritual sense, may now go to the first chapter of Genesis to learn the way of life and salvation.

This immense, and yet, consolidated system of views of God, man and the universe, and of the Holy Word, as the medium of light and life to all created things, strikes many minds, at the first view, as strange and novel; and they turn aside, saying, It is asking too much to request our attention to any such system. But let me ask them if it is asking too much to request their attention to the Word of the Most High God? And let me further ask them what light, from any other philosophy, they can bring to show the use and beauty of the strange things of the Holy Word? Upon what other ground, than this language of analogy, can we possibly account for the propriety or use of many portions of the Sacred Word? What shall we do with the Pentateuch, or with the books of Ezekiel and the Apocalypse, and with many things scattered throughout the Word? Why is the vast universe, in generals and in particulars, so frequently brought before us? The sun, moon, stars, winds, clouds, rain, hail, snow, ice, frost, fire, light, darkness, calms, storms, thunders, earthquakes, floods, droughts, mountains, hills, valleys, seas, rivers, beasts, birds, fishes, reptiles, insects—everything that flies, walks, creeps, swims, or crawls—trees, brambles, briers, shrubs, thistles, plants, wheat, rye, barley, corn—everything that grows upon the earth—gold, silver, copper, brass, iron, lead, precious stones, rocks, clay, sand—everything in the earth; and even the earth itself. Why are these things so frequently mentioned by the Lord, in whole or in part, to teach men the doctrines of the Word and the way of life? for "All scripture is profitable for doctrine." Must it not be because they impart moral and religious instruction by a higher meaning than the letter which killeth? Why are these things mentioned as living and rational creatures? the floods clapping their hands, the hills rejoicing, the trees choosing a king, the mountains moving about, the hills skipping like young sheep, the valleys shouting and singing, the earth reeling to and fro like a drunken man, everything that hath breath praising God, and God entering into covenant with the beasts of the field and the creeping things of the earth; why all this, unless they correspond to principles in man;

so that it is *man* that reels to and fro, *man* that praises God by every living principle of his nature, *man* with whom God entered into covenant, *man* that shouts and sings, *man* that claps his hands, *man* that chooses a king, *principles in man* that skip like young sheep, *mountains in man* that are moved? It must be so: and, by the science of correspondences, it is clearly seen to be so; for all these things are mentioned as "Profitable for doctrine, for reproof, for correction," and "for instruction in righteousness:" that we may be "thoroughly furnished unto all good works." (2 Tim. iii. 16, 17.) But, without this science, what can we learn from such things of the Word as the Lord's shaving with a hired razor, and its consuming the beard from the feet? from the dragon's sweeping down a third part of the stars of heaven with his tail? from a chariot's being cast into a dead sleep? from Jehovah's riding on horseback, or in chariots? from horses coming out of the book when opened? from locusts with shapes like horses, faces like men, hair like women, teeth like lions and tails like scorpions? What can these things mean? Are they the Word of infinite wisdom? They are, most certainly; and they are beaming with truth clear to the mind, and filled with food for hungry souls. Come ye to the banquet! come with confidence and a teachable spirit, and you will find, in every passage, a well of living water, springing up unto everlasting life, for all that are thirsty. How emphatically do all these things point us to nature for the symbol of their true meaning, or for the origin or forms of the words in which divine ideas must be clothed, or expressed, in order to reach human minds on earth. Indeed, it is to nature that we must go for the real basis of all language. However lost we may now be to the true roots and laws of our own dialect, we may soon know, by rational reflection, that it is Dame Nature that has taught us all how to talk. We can lisp only her accents. True, her language has become, to us, much adulterated ; but that is our own fault. We use it nevertheless. Her songs, and shouts, and tears, and groans, and sighs, are the sure expressions of human thoughts and feelings. We can soar only through her eloquence, paint only through her colors, and rejoice only through her gladness. Does any one doubt this ? Then let us inquire into it.

Had we no language, how would we go to work to get one ? Now, think deeply, and seek, as keenly as you can, the answer to this question, and you will find it impossible to see how to express a single idea, in speech, without taking the sign from nature. For illustration.—Had we no words to express the idea of innocence, how would we declare it ? By a harmless expression of the face, a soft tone of the voice, or a gentle motion of the hand ? How should we know but it meant gentleness, kindness, quietude, or some other grace or virtue ? We could not certainly tell. We should have no possible way to definitely express the idea of innocence, without seeking something in nature which was a symbol of innocence. And if we could read the book of nature in correspondences, we should point at once to the lamb ; and that would be our word for innocence. But having lost the science of correspondences, the language we should now draw from nature, if we had none, would be very indefinite. Still, we should go there, for we could get a dialect nowhere else.

But, in the primeval age, when men were good, and saw the qualities of natural things by intuition, they had, at once, something in nature to express every quality and principle of the human mind : for all things correspond to qualities in man, and *name*, by correspondence, signifies quality. And when, in the early days of that golden age, they named the various things of nature according to the different mental qualities which they denoted, they did as men do now, in giving names to new things ; only they acted then from the union of spiritual thought with the natural, and named according to correspondences ; while men now act only from natural thought, and name according to qualities. Thus, we have our *Rocky* and *Green* mountains ; our *White* and *Rattlesnake* hills ; our *Wolf*, *Bear* and *Pleasant* lakes ; our *Crooked*, *Muddy* and *Silver* creeks; our *telegraph wires* and *steam engines*.

We should know that every principle of the understanding and of the will, of the thoughts and feelings, though, in themselves, spiritual things, and entirely above the laws of this lower world, yet, in order to be brought down into natural language for men in the flesh, they must be expressed by natural symbols. For the natural man has no other way, and can think of no other way, to describe his thoughts and feelings but in the use of words which have been drawn entirely from nature. From a moment's reflection, one who has never thought upon the subject, may see that the language he uses to describe his thoughts and feelings, was drawn from nature. Take for instance the whole variety of adjectives by which we express the qualities of mental things ; bitter, sweet, sour, warm, cold, long, short, high, low, dark, light, near, distant, black, white, no matter what. Are they not all taken from the things of this world ? And yet, we use them to describe the states and qualities of the mind. We speak of a *warm* or *cold* heart ; a *bitter, sweet*, or *sour* temper ; a *long, deep*, or *shallow* head ; of *high* or *low* spirits ; a *dark* and *muddy*, or *clear* and *lucid* understanding ; a *bright* or *cloudy* intellect ; a *black* character ; a *distant* relative ; a *near* friend ; a *knotty* subject ; and so we might go on and fill up our discourse. Now, we all know that these words have not the same meaning, when applied to the mind, as they have when applied to matter. We have no proper idea of extension in space when we speak of a long or deep head, or of high or low spirits, or of near and distant relatives ; nor of natural mud or clouds when we speak of a cloudy or muddy intellect ; nor of taste when we speak of a sweet or sour temper. These expressions are used because there is no other way, for persons in the flesh, to speak of spiritual things but through natural symbols ; nor to express the quality of spiritual things but by means of words expressive of the quality of natural things.

And, before the loss of correspondences, a clear spiritual idea was always seen through natural symbols, and was alike understood by all. But when the true law of analogy was lost, this beautiful and certain language fell into mere naturalism, and the Word has since been understood, either precisely as it reads in the letter, or else been considered figurative, and therefore been interpreted according to the various states and prejudices of men. And thence has originated all the different creeds and doctrines of Christendom. And nothing short of the restoration of this science can ever draw out the deep truths of the Word, restore harmony to the minds of Christians, and bring the watchmen to see eye to eye. Nor can this be done by merely bringing the philosophy of this science into the external plane of the mind, so as to see the propriety and consistency of it. Nothing short of the possession of this heavenly light in the affections, and the carrying it out in our lives, will restore order and harmony among men.

But, to accomplish this, it is necessary, in the first place, to have a common plane upon which we can rationally meet to learn the true character of our God, of ourselves and of the way of life, as taught in the Holy Word. This common ground we have, in a light indisputable, in the divine science of correspondences.

But, it is asked, "What is the strongest and most conclusive evidence which you have to offer in proof of the truth and certainty of this new science?" We answer, No evidence can be sufficiently clear and full to satisfy a mind that will not look at it, or that has no taste nor desire for things beyond the gift of this world. But if even such a person were entirely unacquainted with the Chinese language, and should remove to China, and there learn to speak and write that language, so as to read their books and understand them, and should find that they contained a rational and consecutive chain of ideas and history of events, he certainly would be convinced that they had a language, and that he had learned it. It is precisely so with the language of analogy. It must be examined and learned, and tested by the reading of analogical language before it can be understood.

Now let that same man come to the Sacred Scriptures and look at the first two chapters of Genesis, the twenty-fourth chapter of Matthew, the tenth of Ezekiel and the twenty-first of Revelation, and he will be as much at a loss to know their true meaning, as he was that of the Chinese language when he went to that country. But let him learn the language of analogy until he can read and understand the Holy Word by it, and can see a beautiful and consistent course of useful instruction pervading the entire chapters mentioned; and not only them, but also the whole Word, making it a new Book, most clear and instructive, and he will then be much more strongly convinced of the indisputable verity of this language than he was, or could possibly be, of that of the Chinese.

Now, we can say to such persons, that many are the human minds, of different nations of the earth, who are becoming thus convinced. Will not God's Holy Word, then, yet become known as it is, and be universally received, loved and regarded? Will it not become the great Law of the land, and restore universal peace on earth and good will toward men ? It most surely will. That glorious shout of the angels, at the birth of our Lord, was not made in vain. " Behold, I bring you good tidings of great joy, which shall be to all people." (Luke ii. 10.) The Lord, at His second coming, as the light and life of the Word, seen by the law of analogy, will surely bring it to pass. The seals are already broken, and the Holy Spirit is going forth. The pure Truth, or the Lord as the spiritual sense of the Word, is coming in the clouds of heaven, or letter of the Word, into the human mind, with power and great glory ; and every eye shall see Him. Yes, the glorious Bridegroom Himself is coming. Go ye out to meet Him ; go dressed in the wedding garments of the New Jerusalem : go adorned with the precious stones of the Holy City ; with the pearls and rubies of the blessed Word. Yes, let us arise, and go hence, that we may walk the golden streets of the New Jerusalem together, in peace and love. And let us thus hasten on the glorious day when the knowledge of the Lord shall cover the earth as the waters cover the sea ; and when all shall know the Lord, from the least to the greatest. God, by the light of His Holy Word, is offering to us this blessed privilege. Is it worth the reception ? Are heavenly light and life, and peace and joy—are a happy world and a heaven below, and an eternal heaven above worth the attention of men ? Then, I beseech you, let us accept the boon of Jesus' Spirit, and work in His vineyard while the day lasts, that when the final morning of the resurrection comes and we cast off the clay, we may feel in our hearts the warmth and brightness of the rising sun, and hear the plaudit of "Well done, good and faithful servant, . . . enter thou into the joy of thy Lord." (Matt. xxv. 21.)

CHAPTER IV.

THE LAW OF LIFE BETWEEN GOD MAN AND NATURE.

"When Israel went out of Egypt, the house of Jacob from a people of strange language, the sea saw it, and fled; Jordan was driven back; the mountains skipped like rams, and the little hills like lambs." (Ps. cxiv. 1, 3, 4.)

Our subject for this evening is, *The Divine Law of Life between God, Man and Nature.* This law of life is the great law of Analogy. It is the divine rule of action between the Creator and the created. It is the way God gives life to all created things. Life in God is the Divine Love and Wisdom. The Divine Love or Goodness is the essence, and the Divine Wisdom or Truth is the form or manifestation of that Life to man. By the efflux of this Love and Wisdom God created and constantly sustains the universe. But in order for the affectionate reception of this Love there had to be human Will, and for the rational reception of this Wisdom there had to be human understanding.

But this Love and Wisdom could never have been affectionately and rationally received into the human will and understanding without language to teach or express the nature, character and qualities of this divine Life. The only language, in which it could be given, is the language of correspondences, for *that* is the speech of God; and it presents something of that Love and Wisdom in every word it utters. A people who should rationally and affectionately receive that language would know and love God, and possess His image and likeness. A people without any knowledge of it would have no true spiritual idea of God whatever; their thought would be only natural.

That language was once universally understood on the earth, and the world was in true order. And just in the degree that it was lost men lost true ideas of God's nature and character, misunderstood the true doctrines of the Holy Word and divided into various sects, with divers creeds and ceremonies. And when that language is rationally and affectionately received again, by the human family on earth, the world of mankind will be spiritually alive—in the true knowledge and love of God; for it is the eternal Law of Life between God, man and nature. God clearly speaks it in both His Word and His works; and, between the two, the language is definitely explained and rationally taught.

We will therefore now appeal to the Word Itself, in Its analogical connection with nature, in further verification of this law. Now the words *earth* and *heavens* are often used in the Word in such a way as to give no rational instruction, in the literal sense alone, but rather to involve the subject in obscurity, until the true law of life is seen; as where it speaks of the heaven and the earth passing away, and of God's creating a new heaven and a new earth; of the heavens being rolled together as a scroll; of the stars falling from heaven as a fig tree casteth her untimely figs when she is shaken of a mighty wind; or where it says, "The earth mourneth and fadeth away; . . . the earth is utterly broken down, the earth is clean dissolved." (Is. xxiv. 4, 19.) "The earth opened her mouth." (Rev. x. 16.) "The Lord hath forsaken the earth." (Ezekiel ix. 9.) These are strange sayings. But as soon as it is clearly seen that the earth corresponds to man or to the human mind, there may be readily seen something of the beauty and propriety of all such expressions; for if we see that, in the most essential meaning, it is the human mind that is everywhere treated of in the Word, and that it is because the visible world corresponds to that mind, that it is so often mentioned, a most rational light will ever beam from the sacred page where the teaching is otherwise lost in obscurity. Thus we can see that, as the earth is warmed and illuminated by the heat and light of the sun so as to give germination and growth to every living thing upon it, so do spiritual heat and light, which are the love and wisdom of the Lord flowing from Him as the Sun of Righteousness, give germination and growth to every spiritual principle—every good thought and feeling which spring up in the mental earth or soil of the mind. And the cultivation and growth of natural things perfectly correspond to the cultivation and growth of mental things. It is for this reason that there is so much said, in the Word, about breaking up the fallow ground, and sowing, planting, watering, reaping, gathering, and gleaning; and also about thorns, thistles, nettles and briers, as well as wheat, corn and good fruits. For, in the spiritual sense, it is always things of the mental earth which are meant by such expressions; because it is the states and qualities of the human mind that the prophets were all writing about. Thus, in Hosea, the Lord says, "Judah shall plow, Jacob shall break his clods. Sow to yourselves in righteousness, reap in mercy." (x. 11, 12.) "Light is sown for the righteous, and gladness for the upright in heart." (Ps. xcvii. 11.) Man "Soweth discord;" (Prov. vi. 14, 19.) "Soweth strife;" (*ib.* xvi. 28.) Soweth "The wind, and shall reap the whirlwind;" (Hosea viii. 7.) "Soweth iniquity" and "shall reap vanity." (Prov. xii. 8.) The Lord says in Mark, "The sower soweth the Word." (iv. 14.) And in Jeremiah He says, "I will sow the house of Israel and the house of Judah with the seed of man," (xxxi. 27.) by which is meant the truths of the Word, which, if cultivated, will produce the image of God the divine Man. And when the Word is sown it is declared that "Instead of the thorn shall come up the fir-tree, and instead of the brier shall come up the myrtle-tree." (Is. lv. 13.)

Now, as it is in the affections of the human mind that all this sowing and plowing and reaping are done; so also *that* is the place, to which the prophet alludes, when he says, "Thorns shall come up in her palaces, nettles and brambles in the fortresses thereof." (Is. xxxiv. 13.) For the living soul is composed of things good and true in the mind, and when that soul goes down, then the falsities and evils, denoted by thorns, nettles and brambles, come into the heart. Thus it is, that "Thistles come upon" our "altars," because the human heart is the true altar of worship. And *there* it is that the thorns choke the good seed of the Word.

How clear and beautiful is the correspondence between the uncultivated earth and the uncultivated mind! Therefore the cultivation of the earth is often mentioned to denote the cultivation or regeneration of the mind. Thus in Isaiah, speaking of the mind, it says, "I will make the wilderness a pool." (xli. 18.) "Let the wilderness and the cities thereof lift up their voice." (xlii. 11.) "He will make her wilderness like Eden." (li. 3.) This is regeneration. The whole journey of the children of Israel in the wilderness, on their way to Canaan and the expulsion of the Canaanites, is a perfect description, by correspondence, of what every man passes through, in being regenerated. And the degeneration of man is described by the fruitful place becoming a wilderness ;—"The pleasant portions a wilderness." "Edom shall be a desolate wilderness." And as in the natural wilderness are wild and ravenous beasts, so, in a wilderness state of the mind, are savage and head-strong affections and passions to which wild beasts correspond.

We will now mention a few general rules which may be of use to the new student of this divine science. The two great essential principles in God are, love and wisdom. The third principle in Him is power. But this power is the offspring, or rather, the operative force of that love and wisdom. Man's will, in order, corresponds to God's love ; his understanding, to God's wisdom ; and his energy, to God's power. Now, as there is nothing in nature which God's love and wisdom have not brought into being and sustained, and is therefore a direct or perverted image of some principle in Him, it must follow that every natural thing corresponds, in some certain degree, either to goodness and truth or to evil and falsity, in some of their infinite varieties of forms. For, it should be borne in mind that God's love and wisdom are not a unit in goodness and truth, but an infinite variety of goods and truths, all in perfect order and harmony, forming a whole in the Infinite Human form ; and that everything good and true in man or in nature, corresponds to something in the great Form of all forms, from which it derives its existence ; and also that every evil or falsity is a perversion of something in the great divine Being. But this perversion springs from the abuse of man's freedom and not from God. Sometimes the main or prominent correspondence of a thing will be to goodness, yet there will, at the same time, be a certain relation to truth in it. For every good has its truth. And good cannot produce anything without the co-operation of truth, nor can it even exist separate from it. The quality of a thing, generally speaking, has relation to some good or evil ; and its form to some truth or falsity. But, to these general rules, there are exceptions resulting from states or circumstances which will be readily seen as a person progresses in a knowledge and love of this divine science.

Everything that we eat that is wholesome, corresponds to good, and everything that we drink, to truth. Unwholesome things which we eat and drink correspond to evils and falsities. All liquids, as a general rule, correspond to truths or falsities : water to truth or falsity in the natural degree, and wine, in the spiritual degree. Thus, the same thing sometimes corresponds to truth, and at other times to falsity, according to the light in which it is used. But it is readily known to which it corresponds. For, if it be mentioned in a bad sense, as against God's laws and injuring that which is good or true, it would correspond to falsity. But if in a good sense, or according to the divine laws, or as destroying that which is evil and false, it corresponds to truth.

Thus, all the implements of war, used in the battles recorded in Scripture, correspond either to truths or falsities ; those on the Lord's side correspond to truths ; those on the opposite side, to falsities. And even the opposing armies themselves correspond, on the one side, to good principles, and on the other, to evils. Good and evil principles always stand opposed to each other, and their weapons of war are always truths and falsities. Thus the "Sword of the Lord" is the divine truth proceeding out of His mouth ; while the "Sword of the adversary" is falsity.

Water, when it is used in a bad sense, as destroying man, or overflowing lands or cities, or being muddy or bitter, or raging in hail-storms, corresponds to falsity ; but when used in a good sense, as the refreshing shower or gentle dew, the river of God, the pool of Siloam, a well of living water, the water of life, it corresponds to truth. And what a beautiful correspondence to truth is water! It quenches the thirst, cleanses the skin, and performs the same uses to the body which truth does to the mind. In general, all things which are transparent or that reflect images, correspond either to truths or falsities.

The Holy City is said to be "pure gold, like unto clear glass." This is because gold corresponds to goodness and glass to truth; and they are mentioned together to denote the union of goodness and truth. By this we learn that the doctrines of the New Church, in order to become a holy city in our minds, must fill our hearts with their goods and our minds with their truths. Then the doctrines will be clear and beautiful in our minds, They will be pure gold, like unto clear glass.

Again, as the earth corresponds to man, or to the human mind, so all mountains, being the highest parts of the earth, signify the highest or uppermost things in the mind; and these are things of the will—the desires—things which we either warmly love or hate. Therefore, if the thing we most ardently love be goodness, that affection would be called a "Mountain of holiness"—a "Mountain of the Lord." It would be a high state of love to the Lord. This is the mountain which our Savior went up into to pray. For, although He went up into a natural mountain, yet He did it from correspondence; His heart was in love to the Father: His soul was in a mountain as well as His body. Everything He said or did was in correspondences. And He took His body into a mountain to pray to teach us, by outward and expressive acts, that when we pray, we should elevate our affections to God in the highest degree we can. And that we should strive and labor for it mentally, as the Lord did naturally by actually climbing up into a mountain to pray. If the thing we most ardently love be self, manifested in some violent feeling of revenge or malice toward some individual who has injured or slandered us, that bitter feeling is a mountain—the uppermost pinnacle of our mental earth. This mountain must be removed before we can find rest or peace of soul. This is the kind of mountain to which, if we have "faith as a grain of mustard seed," we can say, "Remove hence to yonder place; and it shall remove." (Matt. xvii. 20.) If we have faith to believe that it is wrong to feel unkind toward anybody; that we should love even our enemies, and bless those that curse us, then we can remove this mountain of revenge. But to have faith as a grain of mustard seed, in this case, is to have the blessed truth, which says, "Love your enemies," so deeply sown in the soil of the heart, that it will spring up, for the removal of all such mountains, and become large enough for the birds of heaven, or heavenly thoughts, to lodge in the branches thereof; or, in other words, so that we can think kindly toward our enemies.

Hills, in a bad sense, denote feelings not so high as mountains—not so bitter as revenge or malice—yet, feelings which are unkind and uncharitable. In a good sense, they denote feelings of charity and good-will. From this we may form some idea of what is meant in the Word by the moving about of mountains and hills, as expressed in the text, when "The mountains leaped like rams; and the little hills like lambs," or, more properly rendered, "The sons of the flock." Now, all know that these things could not take place physically; but we readily see that the mountains and hills of the mind may be removed, whether they be good or evil. In the text they were evil. Indeed, we have a singular text, strange enough in the letter. It reads thus, "When Israel went out of Egypt, the house of Jacob from a people of strange language, the sea saw it and fled; Jordan was driven back, the mountains leaped like rams, and the little hills like lambs." What a scene for a mundane eye to behold! But it is spiritual, not natural. And many of us have witnessed something of the kind in our own mental earth.

The sea, in the Word, corresponds to knowledge in general, whether true or false, stored up in the memory. Rivers denote the scientific and doctrinal streams which flow into that sea from study. Places represent states of mind. In our text, by the sea and river are meant false knowledges and doctrines; and by Egypt a state of religious darkness, brought on by a strange language not rationally understood, used in the absence of the pure language of analogy, which had been lost. But let that bright language be again brought clearly into the mind; let Israel and Jacob, which denote divine qualities or the highest religious principles in us, arise and start from their Egyptian mysteries, and look above their strange language by the light of analogy, and, will not the sea of our false knowledges flee?

Will not the river of erroneous doctrines turn back? Will not the mountains of self-love and the hills of the love of the world remove from the affections? Most assuredly they will.

But, it may be asked, how is it that their removal can be so sudden? How can they skip like sheep when they are the very life's love? It is in theory only that they thus leap. The true light shows us the true doctrines; and, intellectually, we see and know that they are true, and that our former views were false and our affections evil. This is quickly done: so that from our *system* of theology all mountains and hills of evil, as they are seen, are, at once, driven to the shades. They leap like rams. When light comes in, darkness must disappear. Thus, our understanding condemns them. But before they can be removed from the natural will, the new light of faith must work by a new love to the Lord, introduced into the internal will by the new light, and thus must purify the natural heart from the love of self. In this way only can those mountains and hills be actually removed. But there is a class of imaginary mountains and hills, in the mind, without foundation, resting on circumstances or on selfish hopes and fears, which are sometimes as suddenly gone as the leaping of sheep. How often do men's high mountains of hope or fear, at once skip from the heart, from some new event of life either blasting every ardent expectation, or quelling all anxious dread! And so of the hills, or imaginary charities. All the natural feelings of kindness and benevolence which exist among men merely from selfish intercourse and enjoyment, and which sometimes seem to be hills of much magnitude and importance, may, by a single reverse of fortune, all skip like young sheep. But God's hills of charity in our hearts, founded in the pure love of mercy and good-will, the reverses of worldly fortune can never disturb. But, on the contrary, they ever magnify them and fill them with new springs of kindness and compassion. It does the generous soul good to pour the oil of sympathy and consolation into the wounds of an afflicted brother.

Valleys, in a good sense, signify the lowest and most external of the affections for either God or the neighbor. In a bad sense, they denote the most base and grovelling affections of the natural mind. But, as all power is in ultimates, so the valleys or externals of the mind, may become immensely productive of good in the community in which we live. There is great natural fruitfulness in the valleys of the earth. The soil of them is luxuriantly fertile. They take the wash of the mountains ; or the mountains give their goodness to the valleys. They also send down their streams to water and refresh them. And with these blessings, with proper cultivation, their productions are abundant. So it is with love, the mental mountain, whether in God or in man. Heavenly love, the mountain of the good soul, wants to give itself away to everything that is below it. It gives of its goodness, and it gives of its truth. And those who, like the valleys, open their bosoms to receive them, and drink in freely the water of life, and partake of the blessings of love, faithfully cultivating the mind, will bring forth much fruit.

Again, the human body is an image of the mind which infills it, and by which it acts ; therefore, every part of the body corresponds to some principle of the mind. It is for this reason that the organs of the body, in regard to both God and man, are so often mentioned in the Word. And by knowing to what principles of the mind the various organs of the body correspond, many, otherwise strange and incomprehensible passages of Scripture, are made plain and instructive. Therefore, when the Lord says, "If thy hand offend thee, cut it off : it is better for thee to enter into life maimed, than having two hands to go into hell." "And if thy foot offend thee, cut it off : it is better for thee to enter halt into life, than having two feet to be cast into hell." "And if thine eye offend thee, pluck it out : it is better for thee to enter into the kingdom of God with one eye, than having two eyes to be cast into hell-fire." (Mark ix. 43, 45, 47.) When the Lord says these things, we are not left in the mazes of darkness, nor in vague conjecture as to what He means. But who would presume to say that the literal sense alone does not leave the subject in profound darkness ? Can any one believe that the natural foot, hand or eye can offend ? Are they not mere instruments of the mind, entirely unconscious, and without responsibility ? But suppose that they could absolutely offend, can we cut them off and cast them from us so that we should be without two hands, feet or eyes in the next life ? Is a man who loses an eye in this life to have but one in the next? It does seem as though it were too late a period in this wonderful age of scientific progression for men much longer, to shut their eyes against this light of analogy. If the Bible is the Word of divine Wisdom, given to man to teach him, it must be intended to be understood. But who, without the science of correspondences, will dare to say that he understands these passages? Surely no humble and pious man would have that presumption. Let us look at them in the light of that science. The hand denotes power or ability. Therefore David prays to the Lord saying, " Send thine hand from above; rid me, and deliver me out of great waters, from the hand of strange children; whose mouth speaketh vanity, and their right hand is the right hand of falsehood." (Ps. cxliv. 7, 8.) Now, who can give any other rational meaning to hands, in this passage, than power; or to waters, than falsities; or to the strange children, whose mouth speaketh vanity, than to evil or the devil who was a liar from the beginning? It is perfectly certain that David here prays that the Lord will send His power from above; and rid him, and deliver him out of many falsities, from the powers of tbe children of the devil whose mouth speaketh a lie, and whose wilful powers are the wilful powers of falsehood. Again, it is written, "His right hand, and His holy arm, hath gotten Him the victory." He conquered, of course, by His power. Hand denotes power; arms, greater power, and shoulders, all power. *If thy hand offend thee, cut it off.* For the hand to offend is to exercise the power and propensity to sin. To cut the hand off, is to cease to exercise that ability, and thus weaken or put away the propensity. We are creatures of habit, and our evil propensities become strong or weak in proportion to the indulgence. In the strength of them is the power or hand. To weaken or put away that strength is called cutting off the hand. The foot, as it is the lower part of the body and most in the dust, denotes the most external and the lowest principle of the mind. For the foot to offend is to indulge in the lowest principle of selfishness. To cut the foot off and cast it from us, is to suspend and mortify that indulgence, till we lose the desire for it.

That the foot denotes the lowest natural principle of the mind, we might know from the one passage alone where our Lord says to Peter, "He that is washed needeth not save to wash his feet, but is clean every whit." Thus teaching plainly that when once spiritually clean, we have only to keep the lower, the outward principles of the mind clean, to be "clean every whit." For it is through the lower principles of our nature that temptations enter, and defile us. Keep this principle pure; guard well this avenue to temptation; keep this door well watched, with the blood of the Lord, or truth of the Word upon its lintel and there is no danger. But, without the spiritual sense, what can the words of the Lord to Peter mean? The Lord was washing the disciples' feet. "Then cometh He to Simon Peter: and Peter saith unto Him, Lord, dost thou wash my feet? Jesus answered and said unto him, What I do thou knowest not now." (John xiii. 6, 7.) Now Peter certainly did know the

Lord was washing the natural feet of the disciples. But he did not know what that act signified. "Peter saith unto Him, Thou shalt never wash my feet. Jesus answered Him, If I wash thee not, thou hast no part with me. Simon Peter saith unto Him, Lord, not my feet only, but also my hands and my head." (xiii. 8, 9.) Then Jesus informed him the feet were all that it was necessary to wash, in order to give the divine instruction conveyed by that act. He wanted to impress upon the world the great importance of keeping the outward acts of life clean; and that they must wash one another's feet, or aid each other in keeping free from outward sins. Who can know, without the spiritual sense, what the Lord meant by saying, "He that is washed needeth not save to wash his feet, but is clean every whit"? For if, after our bodies are washed clean, we keep our feet clean, that will not keep our bodies clean also. Let us then, while we have the spiritual sense, faithfully follow its instructions, and keep the hand and foot from offending: thus shall we be prepared to enter into life.

The eye denotes the understanding. For the eye to offend, is to tell falsehoods and to embrace falsities as truths. To pluck the eye out and cast it from us, is to cease to deceive and to stop trying to reason from fallacies, and to seek for light upon a rational basis until we can reason from correct principles and true doctrines. When we deal in falsehoods, our eye or understanding offends against God, against our neighbor and the laws of our own peace. We must pluck out that false eye by ceasing to deceive, until we love to think and speak from plain truth. And as to its being better to enter into life halt or maimed, or with one eye, rather than having two hands, feet or eyes, to be cast into hell-fire ; that means that it is better to be good and happy here and hereafter in simple truth and virtue, though we cannot know everything and have all power, rather than, by being wise in our own eyes, esteeming ourselves great, and worthy of great power and dominion, we still remain in the love of self, and cast ourselves, with all our boasted wisdom and power, into the fires of envy, jealousy, and malice, and all the attendant miseries of selfishness. The selfish man would think himself spiritually maimed, if his overbearing powers were curtailed. He would think himself halt, if his feet were restrained from their wonted paths of vice. And he would think himself half blind, if not allowed to reason falsely and deceive his neighbors. And the Lord would teach him, by this scripture, that it is better to be happy in what he imagines would be a cramped, mutilated, and imperfect condition, rather than be miserable, in the full possession and indulgence of all his selfish powers and wants. In another view, we may see, that we cannot enter heaven with two eyes, or rather, two understandings ; one dealing in falsities and the other in truths. We cannot go there double-minded, serving two masters. We must have an eye single to the Lord or the truth. Nor can we go there with two hands, or rather, opposite powers of the mind ; one exercised in things evil and the other in things good : nor with two feet, or rather, external opposing natural principles of the mind, one indulging in vices and the other in virtues. We can only go there in singleness of heart, mind and action, led and governed by the Lord. But our spiritual bodies there will be perfect, with eyes, hands, and feet. The cutting of the material body to pieces does not touch the organic structure of the spiritual body. He who loses a limb or an eye, in this world, will not be destitute in the next.

Thus does the Law of Analogy render clear and beautiful, the darkest passages of the Holy Word, and also bring to view new and heavenly light in the most simple and plain portions. We might go on and fill volumes with these illustrations. In fact, I have but slightly touched the spiritual sense of the scripture cited; hinting only at the simplest and plainest correspondences. Much deeper and more wonderful light may be drawn from every passage than we have attempted to evolve. For it is a fountain of infinite Wisdom, known in its fullness only to the most high God; and yet so wisely adapted to men that they can rationally commence the study in the mere twilight of the science; and pursue a path which will grow brighter and brighter to the perfect day. And how emphatically does all this prove to us that the LAW OF LIFE BETWEEN GOD, MAN, AND NATURE, is the sure law of analogy, in which God speaks to us in both His Word and His works! For we thereby receive His love and wisdom—the great elements of eternal life—through a rational knowledge and love of the Divine qualities, given in His language; and which are, in themselves, the life of angels, men and things. Let us then carefully study the sacred Word, as God's first and highest gift to man, as the true medium of eternal light and life to the human soul.

CHAPTER V.

THE CORRESPONDENCE OF BIRDS AND ANIMALS.

"And, thou son of man, thus saith the Lord God; Speak unto every feathered fowl, and to every beast of the field. Assemble yourselves, and come; gather yourselves on every side to my sacrifice that I do sacrifice for you, even a great sacrifice upon the mountains of Israel, that ye may eat flesh, and drink blood. Ye shall eat the flesh of the mighty, and drink the blood of the princes of the earth, of rams, of lambs, and of goats, of bullocks, all of them fatlings of Bashan. And ye shall eat fat till ye be full, and drink blood till ye be drunken, of my sacrifice which I have sacrificed for you. Thus ye shall be filled at my table with horses and chariots, with mighty men, and with all men of war, saith the Lord God." (Ezek. xxxix. 17–20.)

Our present subject is the correspondence of animals and birds to things of the mind, and the use made of them in the Holy Word. And now, let any intelligent person, who has never thought upon the subject, be told that the visible universe corresponds to the human mind, that there is nothing in nature which does not, from its quality and use, denote some principle and quality of the soul of man, let him admit this, and then go rationally and carefully into the examination of nature, for the purpose of finding out what things there, most expressively symbolize human thoughts; and after closely investigating the nature of the vast variety of mundane things, in comparison with human qualities, he will come, most deliberately and decidedly, to the conviction that the birds much more fully and emphatically express man's thoughts, than any other species of things. And for a symbol of human affections, he will select, with the most definite decision, the beast. And the more closely he studies the character and qualities of the various animals and birds, in connection with his own feelings and thoughts, the more strongly will he become confirmed in the belief that there must be some analogical law or connection between the human mind and these creatures. For he will find no quality of the human affections or thoughts which he does not see manifested, to the very life, in the beasts and birds.

Every variety of quality will be there seen, from the most gentle, peaceful, pure, innocent, harmless and affectionate, to the most treacherous, filthy, deceitful, subtle, revengeful, quarrelsome and barbarous. Every shade and tint of man's affections will be found in the beasts, and of his thoughts, in the birds. And he will then see, why the Lord in His Word, is so often bringing forward the beasts and birds to describe the states and qualities of men. He will understand why Herod was called *a fox,* Dan a *lion's whelp* or an adder in the path; and also why the Lord says, "The wolf shall dwell with the lamb, and the leopard shall lie down with the kid: and the calf and the young lion and the fatling together; and a little child shall lead them.

And the cow and the bear shall feed: their young ones shall lie down together: and the lion shall eat straw like the ox." (Is. xi. 6, 7.) He will see by all such language, a beautiful description of the state of the regenerate mind, when all the various feelings of the soul, denoted by the different beasts, are in harmony and love; when the strong lion and leopard of the mind, are filled with the spirit of mercy and truth, and are faithfully protecting the lambs and kids of innocence and virtue, from all harm, and even lying down in their embrace.

He will understand what is meant, in the Word, by the beasts before the throne of God full of eyes before and behind. For as eyes denote the understanding, he will see that it is the affections of man filled with wisdom concerning things future and past. He will also see why it is written that the animals give glory and honor and thanksgiving to the Lord; why the animals say, Amen; why, when the Lord opened the first seal it was a beast that said, "Come and see;" and also, why the beasts fell down and worshipped God, saying, "Amen; Alleluia." He will see that the human heart—the soul's affections—are what is meant by beasts; that it is men and not animals that do these things.

But the novitiate may ask why the birds do not also correspond to the affections, and the beasts to the thoughts, since they both think and feel? We answer, They do, to a certain extent; because thought and affection in man cannot be separated. But to find the full specific difference between the correspondence of beasts and that of birds, to the things of the mind, we must look at the different localities, habits and uses of the two species of creatures ; and also at the correspondence of those localities and habits, to things of the mind. And here we shall find, that the ground, upon which the animals live and walk, and which is dark and opaque, corresponds to the human will ; while the atmosphere, where the birds sing and fly, and which the sun, moon and stars make luminous, denotes the understanding where the light of truth is seen. Then, when we see that the affections, to which beasts correspond, are things of the will, to which the ground corresponds ; and that thoughts, to which the birds correspond, are things of the understanding, to which the atmosphere or firmament corresponds, the question will be settled.

That the ground does correspond to the will, and the atmosphere to the understanding, may be seen, among many other reasons, from the fact, that as truth cannot come into the will but through the understanding, so, neither can light, the correspondent of truth, come to the earth but through the atmosphere. And what is definite in this argument, is, that in the history of the creation, in Genesis, the earth, which denotes the ground of the will, brought forth the beasts ; while water, which denotes truth in the understanding, brought forth the birds. Now, beasts crawl or run on the earth : so move the affections in the will. But birds fly and soar aloft above the earth ; so move the thoughts in the understanding.

Let us now turn our attention more particularly to

the correspondences of birds. And are they not striking symbols of thoughts? How, like the thoughts, they flit about from tree to tree, and object to object, now rising toward heaven and now sinking to earth. One bird meets the eye and is gone. We know not whence he came, nor where he went. How like the coming and going thought! Another appears dressed in beauty. 'Tis like the poet's gilded thought, flying to perch in the verse of fame or affection. Another bird soars, in the morning, on the wings of joy, singing praises to the source of day. It is the grateful Christian's thought, ascending to heaven in the morning anthem.

Some birds descend to the earth to feed upon filth. They are the dissolute thoughts of the grovelling mind indulging in sin. Some are birds of night which cannot bear the light of day. They are the hidden thoughts of the thievish soul, afraid to appear before the eyes of men. Some birds are fierce and cruel, armed with beaks and claws for destruction. They are the malicious murderer's thoughts, seeking carnage and gain. Other birds are as gentle and harmless as the breath of heaven, and as joyous as the music of spring. They are the thoughts of sweet and innocent children, sporting 'mid sunshine and flowers. Some birds, in their union, are as affectionate and as constant to each other as mercy and truth. They are the conjugial thoughts of faithful souls, which no powers can sever, nor adversities weaken. Some birds are as black as darkness, and others as white as the light, while others are mixed with black and white. How perfectly they symbolize, in color, the false, the true, and the adulterated thoughts of men !

Birds are indeed, most true and perfect representatives of thoughts, and throughout the Holy Word, they always denote something of the rational or intellectual element. It is remarkable that almost everywhere, in the Word, where birds are mentioned, some other meaning than the literal sense must be given them before the mind can be satisfied. If we go to the first chapter of Genesis, the very first place where "winged fowl" are mentioned, we are confounded with the idea that the birds were made of water. And we ask if, by any chemical process, they can be reduced to water ? And science answers, No. We ask if their substances have not been changed ? And the Law answers, Everything must bring forth after its kind. The question then arises, Why is it written that the waters brought forth the birds, and the earth the animals ? But this question can never be answered, without the science of correspondences. But when we see that it is a spiritual history and that water, there, corresponds to truth and birds to thoughts, all is light : the mystery is fled. For we see that all the thoughts of the people, before the fall, to which birds correspond, must have been true, for the truths of the Lord brought them forth. And we also see that all the affections, to which the animals correspond, must have been good ; for the will or goodness of God, to which the land corresponds, brought them forth. And as beasts and birds are there used merely for the sake of the spiritual sense, all is rational and clear.

Now, without knowing the correspondence of birds, we cannot know what is meant by its being said in Jeremiah, when prophesying of the coming of the Lord in the flesh (chap. iv. 25), "All the birds of heaven were fled." We are nowhere informed that, at the Lord's first coming, there were not as many birds on the earth as usual. But we know that heavenly thoughts had passed away from the Jewish Church; we know *those* birds of heaven had fled. And therefore, by correspondence, we can understand what is meant. Again, in Isaiah, our Lord says, "As birds flying, so will I defend Jerusalem." In the literal sense of this passage we get nothing; but, in the spiritual sense, we have a general or universal truth. For the Lord never defends a church, or an individual, but as birds flying. It is only by the influx of true thoughts, from the Lord, as birds flying, that we can obtain any true knowledge of the Lord, have true faith, see the way of life, and make a successful defence against our evils. This is the only way the Lord can defend Jerusalem or the Church. When the church in ourselves or in the community is in danger, we must have true thoughts, and we must let them fly from mind to mind, or the church will not be defended. For the Lord expressly says, "As birds *flying*, so will I defend Jerusalem."

And in Jeremiah, our Lord, in speaking of the people of His church, says, "As a cage is full of birds, so are their houses full of deceit." Now what similarity can there be between the deceit of the human mind and a cage full of birds, upon which, even an apology for a metaphor can be founded? Not any. No good sense can be drawn from it, unless we attach a quality to the birds of a deceitful character. But if birds mean thoughts, all is consistent. For thoughts are often deceitful; and their houses would be filled with deceit as a cage or mind is filled with false thoughts.

Again, in Jeremiah, the Lord says, of the people, "How long shall the land mourn, . . . for the wickedness of them that dwell therein? the beasts are consumed, and the birds." (xii. 4.) Now, if, by this passage we understand, by land the good ground of the heart, by beasts the affections, and by birds the thoughts, we shall see the propriety and the use of the teaching. For this was actually the state of the Jewish Church—"the beasts were consumed, and the birds," i. e., good affections and true thoughts were gone or destroyed. But the natural beasts and birds were all on the earth as usual.

And the Lord again says, by the same prophet, "Mine heritage is unto me as a speckled bird; the birds round about are against her." (xii. 9.) Now, why is the church here compared to a *speckled bird?* Is not a speckled bird as good as any other? And, why is it said that the other birds are against the speckled one? Do the birds of this world fight the speckled ones more than others? It is impossible to draw any rational instruction from this passage without coming to the spiritual sense. But all is clear if we call the speckled bird an adulterated state of the mind, by mixing up truths and falsities together; the white spots indicating truths, and the black ones falsities, so that the thoughts are presented, partly true and partly false—a speckled bird. True thoughts would then be against her on account of her falsities ; and false ones, on account of her truths—the birds round about would be against her. A church, or a professed Christian, must be true, or the people round about, or out of the church, will condemn him—the community will be against a speckled bird.

In Revelation, speaking of the church as a city, or rather, as to doctrines, it says, "Babylon the great is fallen, is fallen, and is become the habitation of devils, and the hold of every foul spirit, and a cage of every unclean and hateful bird." (xviii. 2.) Here is described a fallen and depraved state of the mind. Devils and foul spirits belong to minds and to false doctrines, not to natural cities. And there too dwell all unclean and hateful thoughts, not natural birds. How true it is that a fallen and corrupt mind is a cage of such birds !

In the 39th chapter of Ezekiel we have the strange words of our text. "And thou son of man, thus saith the Lord GOD ; speak unto every feathered fowl, and to every beast of the field, Assemble yourselves, and come ; gather yourselves on every side to my sacrifice that I do sacrifice for you, even a great sacrifice upon the mountains of Israel, that ye may eat flesh, and drink blood. Ye shall eat the flesh of the mighty, and drink the blood of the princes of the earth, of rams, of lambs, and of goats, of bullocks, all of them fatlings of Bashan. . . . . . Thus ye shall be filled at my table with horses and chariots, with mighty men, and with all men of war, saith the Lord GOD." Now, whoever looks into this wonderful passage of Holy Writ, and believes it to be the Word of God to man, and "profitable for doctrine," must come to the conclusion that God either has given, or will yet give to man, some rule or law other than the literal meaning, by which its true signification may be understood. If he has not come to this conclusion, he is in doubt about its ever being understood, with any degree of certainty, or even of its being the Word of God at all. If any one does not believe what I say, let him faithfully examine the passage without the aid of correspondences, and see if I have not met his case.

A person may give his assent to a thing without weighing it, and think he believes, when he really knows nothing about it. No faith is worthy the name where the believer does not rationally see something of the truth of what he believes. And all who are acquainted with the science of correspondences, well know, that the above quotation from Ezekiel cannot be understood without the light of that science. What sort of chariots can they be which every feathered fowl and every beast of the field are to be filled with at this feast? By what rule of metaphor can be drawn any rational conclusions from the declaration that the beasts and birds, by eating the flesh of the mighty, and drinking the blood of the princes of the earth, of rams, of lambs, of goats and of bullocks, will thereby be filled, at the Lord's table, with horses and chariots, with mighty men and all men of war? But when the correspondences of beasts and birds, horses and chariots, flesh and blood, princes and mighty men, and rams, lambs, goats, and bullocks, are seen, then the passage becomes divine Scripture, profitable for doctrine.

This passage treats, prophetically, of the establishment of the church in the mind of man, by the Lord, at His second coming. The assembling together of every feathered fowl, and every beast of the field, means, the bringing of all the thoughts and affections into harmonious contemplation of the Holy Word and of the Lord's will; and by eating flesh and drinking blood, means for these thoughts and affections to appropriate to themselves divine good and divine truth; for flesh signifies good and blood truth. Chariots denote doctrines, and horses, the understanding of doctrines; so that to be filled with horses and chariots, is to understand and receive the doctrines. The flesh and blood of princes and mighty men, and of rams and lambs, and goats and bullocks mean, goods and truths from the Lord through others; for these beasts denote good affections. We receive goods and truths through each other. When persons love these goods and truths and love each other, they give and receive these heavenly blessings. The rams and lambs, and goats and bullocks, mean the various good affections of the people, through which they impart to each other the goodness and truth of the Lord.

How beautifully and forcibly are we here called upon, by the Lord, to call together at His Holy supper, or whenever we come into social worship, all our affections and thoughts, or beast and birds, that they may feast upon the goods and truths of heaven, the flesh and blood for our souls, freely imparted from heart to heart and from mind to mind, until our understandings are filled with the heavenly doctrines, or with horses and chariots ; and our hearts overflow with love and good will. In this blessed way the whole beclouded book of Ezekiel becomes, by this divine science, a free and open fountain of living water—a river flowing from the throne of Jehovah—a city whose gates are ever open, emitting a light and heat which reach both the head and the heart.

That chariots denote doctrines, a little fair examination must convince any one. In the Psalms we have this apparently strange expression : "At thy rebuke, O God of Jacob, both the chariot and horse are cast into a dead sleep." (lxxvi. 6.) Now, that a chariot could not be put to sleep, is certain. But, that doctrines could become passive in man's mind, and even pass into forgetfulness, is also certain. And in our text it is seen that birds and beasts could not be filled with chariots ; but that thoughts and affections can be filled with doctrines.

We read of chariots of fire, but we can have no rational idea of such things, literally. But when we know that chariot means doctrines, and fire love, we have something for the mind to feed upon. For the doctrine of love or of life, is a heavenly doctrine. And by this knowledge we can see why it was that Elijah and Elisha were called the chariots of Israel and the horsemen thereof. For they who have the doctrines of the church in their understandings and live them, are mentally, the chariots of Israel and the horsemen thereof. It is because Elisha loved the doctrines of the Holy Word and had them in his understanding that there were seen a chariot and horses of fire when Elijah went up by a whirlwind. For *chariot of fire* means doctrine of love. Were we progressing rapidly toward the heavenly state, by the doctrines of love to God and the neighbor, our spiritual state would correspond to chariots of fire. And the laws of the spiritual world are such that a person, with his spiritual eyes opened, would behold the state of our mind, by seeing near us, chariots of fire.

This was what the young man, mentioned in 2 Kings, saw, where it is written, "And Elisha prayed, and said, LORD, I pray thee, open his eyes that he may see. And the LORD opened the eyes of the young man; and he saw: and behold, the mountain was full of horses and chariots of fire round about Elisha." (vi. 17.) Otherwise, what does this passage mean? Could there be such things as horses and chariots of fire in this world? Yet, the understanding could be filled with the doctrines of the Word and they could be ardently loved. And that state of mind would correspond to horses and chariots of fire. I am aware that it seems very strange to the natural mind that these states and qualities of the mind should be manifested in form, in the spiritual world. But, how can the qualities of things be seen without form to manifest them?

Everything in the other world is mental. It is a world of mind—a world of spiritual bodies, and of thoughts and feelings. And if we could not see their forms, there would be no scenery there. It is the same world that we have here, only here it is clothed with matter. Therefore the things here correspond to things of the mind. Now, that a chariot should be the manifest form of doctrine, may be quite rationally seen by comparative illustration ; but to be truly and clearly seen, we must behold it in the light of correspondence. To illustrate by comparison :—a chariot is composed of various parts, harmoniously put together, forming a whole. Its use is to carry our natural bodies on a natural journey. Doctrines consist of various principles of truth, all harmoniously arranged, for the rational conception of the human mind ; calculated to enlighten, elevate, and give spiritual progress to the mind that receives them. Thus they constitute a spiritual chariot. To behold this chariot, is to see the doctrines ; to get into it, is to love them ; and to ride in it, is to live them. And as we ride on, the chariot itself becomes more and more beautiful, presenting new combinations and arrangements of principles and parts, making it more and more perfect and heavenly. For the deeper and more hidden excellencies of its internal qualities are constantly presenting themselves. We are struck with the beauty of the leading outlines of this chariot, when we first get a fair view of the Trinity, Atonement, Fall, regeneration, resurrection, judgment, &c. Every part is so perfectly fitted to the others. All is symmetry and harmony. We know that *this* chariot will run well : for the truths are seen by their own light, and become self-evidently true.

Now, the Lord is often said, in the Word, to ride in chariots. But, who can know what it means, unless he knows that chariots mean doctrines? If he knows this he has something tangible and definite in the instruction. For he can see that the Lord can come to us in doctrines. And he may know that He does so come. When we behold the doctrines of the New Church from an affection for them, they become to us fixed and eternal verities. They are seen in their own light, and become the indisputable evidence of their own truth, because they are *felt* as well as seen to be true. Therefore they become a chariot that we feel safe to ride in. We are not afraid of losing a wheel, nor of being upset or thrown over a precipice in the end. And if our horses are well trained and governed; that is, if our understanding of the doctrines be clear; and we keep the bit well watched, or keep the understanding from breaking over the rules of the Holy City and running wild, our journey to the promised land, in this chariot, will be not only safe but highly delightful.

In the 7th verse of the 20th Psalm we read, "Some trust in chariots, and some in horses; but we will remember the name of the LORD our God." Here, "chariots" denotes false doctrines, and "horses" self-derived intelligence. And we must not trust in these; but in the qualities of the Lord. For name signifies quality; and God's qualities are goods and truths. For by chariots are not always meant true doctrines, nor by horses, truth in the understanding. These, as well as other things, have their opposite signification. As in Ezek.

xxvi. 7, 8, 10, 11, "Behold, I will bring upon Tyrus Nebuchadrezzar, king of Babylon, a king of kings, from the north, with horses, and with chariots, and with horsemen, and companies, and much people. He shall slay with the sword thy daughters in the field: and he shall make a fort against thee. . . . By reason of the abundance of his horses their dust shall cover thee; thy walls shall shake at the noise of the horsemen, and of the wheels, and of the chariots, when he shall enter into thy gates, as men enter into a city wherein is made a breach. With the hoofs of his horses will he tread down all thy streets: he shall slay thy people by the sword, and thy strong garrisons shall go down to the ground." Here we have a prophecy of the destruction of the church, or of the principles of good and truth in the people. The king of Babylon is falsehood in dominion: his chariots and horses are false doctrines in the understanding. The north, from which he comes, is darkness. Daughters mean good principles; and the field means the affections or will. So that, to slay the daughters of the field, is to destroy the good qualities of the mind. The walls, which are shaken and the garrisons thrown down, are the doctrines destroyed. The sword which he uses is falsehood against the truth. The dust with which he covers the people, is the lowest and most external naturalism.

What a Fountain of wisdom we have before us, in the Holy Word, as opened by correspondences! Let us not despair because it is infinite, nor because we cannot comprehend more of it at once. Think of how much more we know, than we did before we saw this light. And remember that the Teacher is infinite. Jesus will ever help us in the study of His Word if we look to Him. It is truly He that opens the book, for a clear and satisfactory vision.

First; we have the light of the science of Theology presented to our natural reason, so that we begin to see its philosophy by a new and heavenly law. If we apply it to our hearts, in obedience to the truth, the books of our own understandings will be opened by the spirit of Jesus: all doubts will flee away, and we shall go on the heavenly way together rejoicing, in new light and new life. Every day will bring us something new, and a new appetite to enjoy it. Love growing warmer, friendships stronger, the Lord more lovely and heaven more bright.

CHAPTER VI.

THE SYMBOLIC MEANING AND USE OF HORSES.

"And I saw heaven opened, and behold a white horse; and He that sat upon him was called Faithful and True, and in righteousness he doth judge and make war. And the armies which were in heaven followed him upon white horses, clothed in fine linen, white and clean."—Rev. xix. 11, 14.

WHAT a scene for heaven! The Most High God, the Creator of the universe, marshalled at the head of mighty armies, all upon snow-white horses, and clothed in fine linen, white and clean: and this Infinite Commander, leading the countless hosts to battle; with a sharp sword going out of His mouth; His eyes as a flame of fire, and His head surmounted with crowns upon crowns, many in number; with the significant motto upon his vesture and thigh, KING OF KINGS AND LORD OF LORDS! What a scene of sublimity! How awfully grand and exciting even to natural thought! But we are not enough awake to truly imagine its grandeur. Could we peer, with our natural vision, into the open firmament and behold such a scene, how utterly we should be lost in wonder and dismay! Such a magnificent army of horsemen, with an Almighty Commander, all upon such proud, white steeds, rushing through the vaulted skies to battle, would be completely overwhelming to every earthly beholder!

Yet this is the plain literal description, given in the sublime language of Jehovah, of a spiritual scene which we may all realize and enjoy. A scene which will prove equally wonderful and captivating to our souls; for it will open our minds to a clear understanding of the nature of this divine warfare, present us with beautiful white horses, enable us to join the mighty armies of heaven, and to follow the Great Commander on to victory and glory. But as it is a spiritual scene, he who would behold it, must find it in the human mind. The heaven which John saw opened, and where he beheld these wonders, was that heaven which "cometh not with observation," it is not "Lo, here, nor lo, there," but within the human mind.

Let us then turn our thoughts inward to the proper field of action, that we may learn the divine lesson taught in the text; and join the armies of heaven; and fight the battles of Jehovah, like faithful soldiers of the cross. But how can we learn this divine lesson? We must learn it, in humble dependence upon the Lord, through the light of the divine Truth; by looking through the natural symbols of the Word, up to the spiritual realities; remembering that "the invisible things of God from the creation of the world are clearly seen, being understood by the things that are made." But, what invisible things can we behold in the human mind through the symbol of a white horse?

In that symbol, we may see represented, the truth of the Word in man's understanding. How can we know, beyond a doubt, that a white horse denotes the understanding of the truth? We may know it from the study of the symbols of the Holy Word; for therein God clearly teaches it by correspondence.

The Book of Nature and the Holy Word are God's two great books. Both speak the same language—the language of divine and human thoughts and feelings. But *man's* words, in *this* age are arbitrary signs of ideas. We must first learn their definitions, and keep them in the memory, before we can know what ideas they signify. But God's words contain their definitions in their qualities. And we should see them there if we were spiritually minded. Words are called signs of ideas. Now, all the things of nature are signs of ideas. They are living signs of living ideas, and they must bespeak, by their life and quality, the ideas which formed them and which constantly give them life and character. Indeed, there can be no other pure language—no other full and perfect signs of ideas—no other certain expression of the various qualities of human souls, than the symbols of nature. For the human mind constantly receives life from the Lord, and that life flows down through man into nature, carrying with it the qualities of the human passions and propenities; and thus making nature, at all times, a symbol of humanity as it is.

Now, all language was drawn from the things of nature. "There is no speech nor language where their voice is not heard." But men have perverted and corrupted the true language, in thousands of ways, until they have lost sight of the real symbol, and see not the law of correspondences. They know not that the human mind is perfectly symbolized in nature, and that our thoughts and feelings, and all the various qualities of our souls, can be accurately described in no other language ; and that the language of the Holy Word is, therefore, written in the speech of nature, by a universal law; and could be perfect and divine in no other language. Did the world see this, the ten thousand apparently strange and mysterious things of the Word, would soon lose their mystery, and open their heavenly treasures of light and life, to the souls of men. Then men would look into nature's significant mirror for a view of their mental qualities. And they would there behold

Their Thoughts symbolized in the Birds,
" Innocence " " " Lambs,
" Watchfulness and Combativeness in the Dogs,
" Selfishness and Indolence " " Hogs,
" Slyness and Artifice " " Foxes,
" Malice and Cruelty " " Wolves,
" Subtleness and Sensuality in the Serpents, and
" Understanding of Knowledge in the Horses.

And so they might go on with their investigations, until they gained full possession of the lost key of analogy, which unlocks the divine casket of heavenly wisdom, and opens to the human mind, the spiritual truths of the Holy Word, in great glory and beauty.

But in this discourse we must inquire particularly

into the correspondence and use of the horse, in the Divine Word. The Holy Word speaks much of horses, where every one must see that it cannot mean natural horses ; but must, in the divine language, mean something of the human mind. Now, if we will only admit that the term *horse* means the understanding of knowledge, and read the Word with that idea in the mind, connected with other correspondences, all the strange passages of the Word, where the term horse is used, will be rationally understood. But if we should adopt any other signification, the passages could not be understood. We could make nothing out of them.

The Word speaks of horses and their riders. The horses signify knowledge in the understanding, or the understanding of things, whether true or false. The riders are the persons themselves, who have this understanding and knowledge. If I have the truth in my understanding, my knowledge or understanding of that truth performs the same uses for my mind, that a horse does for my body. For by the knowledge of that truth, my mind travels or advances. If it be scientific truth, it carries me on in science. If it be spiritual truth, it takes me on my spiritual journey, as a horse takes me on a natural journey. By the divine truth in our understanding, we perform the heavenly journey, passing around the mountains of sin, through the valleys of humility and repentance, along the streams of science, over the hills of charity and kindness, drinking at every crystal fountain of wisdom, avoiding the bogs and marshes of iniquity, and the thorny jungles of vice ; crossing the pleasant plains of peace and plenty, till we find our heavenly home in the top of the Mountain of the Lord, or in love to God and the neighbor.

Without the understanding of divine truth, we could not possibly make spiritual progress. We rest and rely upon the understanding and power of the truth, as we rest and rely upon the ability and strength of our horse ; and there is a perfect correspondence between them. For the natural purposes, for which we use the horse, are perfectly analogous to the spiritual purposes for which we use our knowledge of the truth.

Now, if, instead of the truth, our understanding be filled with false, absurd, and evil views, it will be like a wild, frantic, ungovernable horse, leaping all the fences or rules of law and order, starting at every new object, getting into mud and mire, and often jeopardizing our life on the way. A man with such a mind needs to keep a strong bit and a straight rein over his headstrong understanding, or it will surely run away with him, and throw him among the rocks of error, on the wayside of destruction, or down the precipice of vice.

Now, all the qualities of the horse prove the truth of this correspondence. His strength denotes the powers of our intellect ; his speed, the activity of our thought ; his great memory, our powers of recollection ; and, his sagacity, our quickness of perception.

But now, to the law and the testimony for the proof of these things. The Lord, in prophesying of the future dark state of the church, says, through Zech. xii. 4, " In that day, saith the LORD, I will smite every horse with astonishment, and his rider with madness: and I will open mine eyes upon the house of Judah, and will smite every horse of the people with blindness." This prophecy has reference to the state of the Jewish church when the Lord should come in the flesh. Now, this prophecy is fulfilled; and we know that every natural horse was not smitten with astonishment and blindness; while we, at the same time, know that the understandings of the Jews became astonished, and were blind to the truths of the gospel; and that they remain so to this day.

Again, it is declared in Genesis xlix. 17, "Dan shall be a serpent by the way, an adder in the path, that biteth the horse heels, so that his rider shall fall backward." Now, all see at once, that this can have no reference whatever to a natural serpent or horse. But we may also see that the debasing principle in man, to which the serpent corresponds, would, by its poisonous bite, soon sicken and destroy the understanding of truth, to which the horse corresponds, and prostrate the rider in sin.

In Habakkuk (iii. 8, 15) it is written, "Thou [Lord] didst ride upon thine horses, thy chariots of salvation. Thou didst walk through the sea with thine horses." Now, all know that the Lord does not ride through space on natural horses, nor in chariots, nor in the natural sea. For He is the Omnipresent God—everywhere at all times. But if the sea denotes man's knowledge; horses his understanding; chariots, doctrines; and the Lord, the Word of truth, the passage becomes exceedingly beautiful and instructive.

For, with the Lord as the divine truth, in the understanding, we can ride through the sea of our memory, examine all the qualities of our knowledge, and make that sea give up its dead ; or cast away all its false and evil principles. Thus the Lord, as the Truth, rides on the horses of men's understanding, or enables them to progress in wisdom and goodness. And so it is that the Lord rides in the chariots of salvation, or in the doctrines of the Word. For the Lord is the Truth of those doctrines. And men's understandings of that truth are the horses of those chariots. And those who love and daily live in obedience to those heavenly doctrines, through the truth of them in the understanding, are riding with the Lord, in the chariots of salvation. They are progressing heavenward with the Word of Truth. Thus, the darkness of the letter is everywhere made luminous by the brightness of the spirit.

Who can tell, from the literal sense, why Elijah and Elisha were called the *chariots of Israel and the horsemen thereof.* (2 Kings ii. 12 ; xiii. 14.) And yet, the doctrines and truths of the Word, in their understandings, as prophets of the Lord, would make them, spiritually speaking, the chariots of Israel and the horsemen thereof. The Lord in Psalms is said to *ride on the Word of Truth.* Why so? Simply because, by the Word of Truth in the understanding, man makes spiritual progress, when he looks to the Lord to curb and guide that understanding in the use of that Word of Truth.

In Psalm lxxvi. 6, we have this apparently strange

expression: "At thy rebuke, O God of Jacob, both the chariot and horse are cast into a dead sleep." We, of course know that there can be no such thing as the waking or sleeping of a natural chariot. But if we have false views and false doctrines in our understandings, our mental horse and chariot need the rebuke of the Lord. And if we yield to that rebuke, they will be cast into a dead sleep, and laid aside as useless.

Now the Word speaks of *White Horses, red horses, Black horses* and *pale horses.* But the color of the horse always denotes the quality of the knowledge in the understanding. A white horse signifies true knowledge, or truth in the understanding, because white denotes truth. A black horse signifies false knowledge, or falsehood in the understanding, because black denotes falsehood. A red horse in a bad sense, signifies guilty knowledge, or crime and evil in the understanding, because red in a bad sense, denotes sins. A pale horse signifies lifeless knowledge in the understanding, or knowledge having no strength or power of good, because paleness denotes sickness or death.

Now, all these kinds of horses are mentioned in the Word, where they can in no light whatever, mean natural horses. For these four horses are mentioned in the sixth chapter of Revelation, as coming out of the Book when the seals were opened by the Lord. And though this prophecy relates to the last judgment in the spiritual world; yet, let us apply it to ourselves individually, for all Scripture is applicable to individuals.

Now, the books which are opened at the Lord's second coming, are nothing else than the Holy Word and the books of life in human minds. The understandings of men are opened to the reception of the light of the spiritual sense of the Word. The understanding of this sense is really the white horse seen in the book of the human mind. This sense in the mind, is the Lord on a white horse ; or, in other words, it is the spiritual truth of the Word in the understanding, coming to judgment. This white horse is seen at the breaking of the first seal, or when our mind first begins to receive, by correspondence, the spiritual sense of the Word in a rational light. Then, our understanding of the spiritual truth is the white horse. The new truth looks pure, white, glorious to us. And we behold the heavenly doctrines with great joy and delight. And we feel as though heaven were indeed near to us.

But we have only been gazing outwardly at the glory and beauty of the truths ; and have not yet looked, by their light, in upon our evils. And the Lord now opens His Word still further to our mind, which opens the second seal of our book of life, and we begin to look into ourselves, in judgment ; and what do we see ? Alas ! *a red horse !* Our understanding is now filled with a view of our own evils. Our sins are before us, red as crimson. But the rider on the white horse, who entered our mind at the opening of the first seal, had a bow, which denotes power : and a crown was given Him, which denotes victory and dominion : and He went forth conquering and to conquer. Thus we have a bow and a crown offered to us by this heavenly truth, which means that the Lord will give us power to gain dominion over our evils. For the Lord Himself is with us, with the crown of His wisdom and the bow of His might. And, notwithstanding the formidable appearance of the red horse and his mighty rider, with his great sword, and power to take peace from the earth ; yet we can, with our white horse, ride on, conquering and to conquer : we can overcome every evil.

Then another seal of our book of life is opened ; and, as we look in, behold a *black horse* presents himself, with a rider having a pair of balances in his hand. Our understanding is now filled with a view of our falses. By the spiritual light, we see our own selfish proprium, separate from what God gives us, and it is all deceitfulness and untruth—black with dissimulation. We even see a pair of balances in our hand, which we are holding out to make the world believe we are honest and just. But, in our dependence upon the Lord, we can surely rout the black horse and his rider ; or the falsehoods and powers of the natural man ; but we must see that they hurt not the oil and the wine, or things good and true.

And the fourth seal of our book of life is opened, and as we survey our selfhood closely, by the divine light, we behold a *pale horse,* whose rider is death ; and hell follows with him. It is a sad picture. Thus the book is opened gradually. We are not permitted to see ourselves all at once. Here, at the opening of this seal, we are brought to see ourselves as dead in trespasses and sins. As having no good whatever of our own; that death and hell are in every unregenerate human soul; that everything good and true is of and from the Lord; and that we shall receive them, only as we conquer and overcome our evils, by new life from the Lord, in obedience to His Word.

Thus the Lord, as the divine Truth of the Word in its spiritual sense, is coming to judgment. He comes with the law of analogy and the philosophy of life; and with them He opens the seals of our understanding and presents, to the free inquiring mind, a rational view of human nature, at this age of the world, in all its evils and falses. And how graphic the description and humiliating the scene! How it tries the heart and the reins, as we see and feel the force of its truth! And yet, he who sees and feels it, is ready to say, "Even so, come Lord Jesus:" for he sees his selfishness, and feels his dependence.

And how orderly the book is opened! After the reception of the White Horse, or when we have seen, by the spiritual truth of the Word, a glimpse of its glorious doctrines, and commence looking into ourselves; we first, by that light, behold our evils and their powers, expressed by a red horse and his rider; next, our falses and their powers, by a black horse and his rider; and then, our state of death and hell, by a pale horse and his rider. In the red and black horses, we see great strength and power. We see depicted all the energy and force of the hells. While in the pale horse, we see our own weakness and entire inability.

Now as the pale horse comes after the red and black

ones, we are further taught that spiritual death and hell are produced by the exercise of evil affections and false thoughts; and that, consequently, life and heaven can be given, only in the exercise of good affections and true thoughts. And that these can be received from the Lord, only as we ride the white horse with the bow of the Holy Spirit and the crown of victory; going forth against our evils and falses, conquering and to conquer; acknowledging, at the same time, that it is truly the Lord and *His* bow and *His* crown, that gain the victory.

But dark and depraved as the picture of our soul appears, we are not to be discouraged. For the opening of the fifth seal shows us the good things which the merciful Lord has stored up and protected within us. As that seal is opened it is said that we see, under the altar, the souls of them that were slain for the Word of God; and that white robes were given them. Now what can this mean? Like all other things of the Word, we must look within for them; for souls are elements of life given us by God. And when we use this Scripture, as applied to ourselves individually, these souls that were slain for the Word of God mean all the good and kind germs of heaven which were implanted in us during our infancy and childhood; and which, though they have been slain and buried by our disorderly lives, yet, are not destroyed. The merciful Lord has guarded them. And now the divine goodness and truth flow down into them, and white robes are given them. They rise to life and shine with the truth. Thus all the honest, true, virtuous, and affectionate principles of our whole life, which have sprung from these germs, and yet have been lying dormant for want of light, but which were internally regarded by us, are now separated from our evils, and raised to light and life. Nothing good is lost. And we are now enabled to see, by the heavenly light, that while, in and of ourselves, we are spiritually dead ; yet, that the Lord is light and life for us. That He has freely given to every one all the germs and elements of heaven. And that He guards and protects these germs and elements of heaven with all care ; but that they can never be developed into a human soul, of angelic form and beauty, without our coöperation. That the goats, in us, must be separated from the sheep, by our free opposition to them, and be cast out of the fold. And that every principle which God has given us—all the lambs of the fold—must look to the Good Shepherd for sustenance, and obey His voice.

And now the sixth seal of our book of life is opened. And as we look in, we behold, exhibited, our dark religious views before we saw the spiritual light. We see the false ideas we then had of God ; of the trinity ; of the fall ; of redemption ; of regeneration ; of resurrection ; of judgment ; of heaven ; and of hell. We behold, in the light of heavenly truth, the whole picture in its own dark colors. And we see it to be contrary to the whole Word of God, in its true literal and spiritual senses. And it is declared in the prophecy that, at the beholding of this scene, "there was a great earthquake ; and the sun became black as sackcloth of hair, and the moon became as blood ; and the stars of heaven fell." This graphic picture describes the appearance of our former system of faith, as seen in the light of truth. And we now behold it as without sun, moon or stars; entirely destitute of all true light and life. It trembles and quakes before the light of truth. And with astonishment, that we ever could have believed it, we roll it together as a scroll, and put it out of sight. Thus, the imaginary heaven of our former theology, passes away from our mind, and we turn our faces, with renewed joy and delight, toward the new heaven, which God is creating within us; where all is light and glorious in the Lord; and only our remaining evils and falses look dark. For we are now closing and putting by our old book of life, with all that we believed and loved that is false and evil, and retaining all that is good, and are turning to the new book of love to God and man. Now, an entirely new theology is filling our heart and mind. Old things with us are passing away, and the Lord is making all things new. The New Jerusalem is coming down; and we are preparing to join the armies of heaven that follow the Lord on white horses, clothed in fine linen, white and clean. For this great army comprises those who have the spiritual truth of the Word in their understandings. And their white horses are nothing but the understanding of that truth. And their white clothing is nothing but the pure, spotless character which their love and devotion to the truth manifest in their sphere. Their warfare is against nothing but the evils and falses which infest humanity, destroying all true peace and happiness. The horse of their Commander is nothing but their own understanding of the truth of the Word. It is therefore not a horse out of their minds, but in them. And the Commander Himself—the "King of kings and Lord of lords"—is that very divine truth of the Word. He is, therefore, not their commander *out* of them, but *in* their understandings; though He fills the universe.

And the many crowns which He wears are a crown each, for every mind He enters. And it becomes an ensign of victory to the man that wears it as he, through the Lord, conquers the death and hell of his soul. And the crown itself, is nothing but the dominion which truth gains over his evils and falsities. And the sharp sword, which went out of the Lord's mouth, is nothing but the divine truth, which He speaks. But it is indeed a sharp sword against everything impure and unholy, going forth for their eternal dispersion and destruction, from every heart that wields it.

And it is our blessed privilege, in the spiritual light of the Word which we now have, to make use of this divine sword as true and faithful soldiers of the cross. King of kings and Lord of lords therefore means, the Lord Jesus Christ as the divine truth of the Word, with power and great glory, coming to establish His kingdom over all the earth, by entering all human minds that will receive Him; presenting them with the bow of His power and the crown of His might; and riding on with them, in their understandings, conquering and to conquer, until every evil spirit shall be driven from our earth, and every sinful desire subdued among all nations and kindreds and tongues and people : when peace shall rest in every bosom, joy beam from every face, and plenty crown every board. And then, in view of the future life, the departure from this world will be cheerfully welcomed by every individual, whenever it shall please the Lord to say to that individual, *Come.* Come, my child. Come home to your Father's house of many mansions. "Thou hast been faithful over a few things, I will make thee ruler over many things : enter thou into the joy of thy Lord." (Matt. xxv. 21.)

CHAPTER VII.

THE CORRESPONDENCE OF TREES.

"The thistle that was in Lebanon sent to the cedar that was in Lebanon, saying, Give thy daughter to my son to wife." (2 Kings xiv. 9.)

WE speak this evening upon the spiritual meaning of trees, and their relation to the human mind by correspondences. A person who has never examined the Holy Word with regard to the signification of the trees and their use in the divine language, would be much surprised and benefited by a candid and sincere investigation of this subject. How few persons there are, even of those who read the sacred volume, who are really aware that the trees are treated of as though they were rational beings, having understandings and wills and muscular powers, so that they walk and talk and laugh and sing and worship and rejoice and clap their hands; are sometimes in great happiness, and at others, in great misery; now strong, and now weak even to fainting; one day in an Eden of glory, and the next going down to hell.

To those who look not beyond the literal sense of the Word, such things are little noticed when read. The meaning not being seen, no impression is left on the mind ; and the reader is hardly sensible that the Word contains any such ideas. Thus a great portion of the Holy Word is of but little use to such minds. For where no rational and practical meaning is seen in the letter, the deeper and more glorious spirit, the inner beauty and excellence, must be brought out to view, or the mind will be left uninterested and uninstructed : and the sacred Word will lose much of its value and influence.

What can the literalist learn from our text ? He will say, it is figurative. And there he must stop if he sees not the law of analogy. He may guess, and guess again; but he cannot certainly know why the Lord said, "The thistle that was in Lebanon sent to the cedar that was in Lebanon, saying, Give thy daughter to my son to wife ;" for, to know this, he must know what principles in the mind are meant by the natural things mentioned.

And so David says in prayer, "Purge me with hyssop and I shall be clean ;" and we, in our worship repeat the same prayer. But *we* are privileged to know, by the spiritual light of the word, that by hyssop is meant external truth, which is a means of purification. And when we say, "Purge me with hyssop," we mean, *Cleanse me with truth.* But, without the science of correspondences, whose eye beholds this passage and attaches any positive or certain signification to hyssop ? Yet how interesting it must be, to one who is thirsting for the pure water of life, to know definitely what the Lord means when He speaks. But. how can we know that hyssop denotes natural truth? If we were far enough advanced to see the relation between natural things and mental, we should know at once. But not having that knowledge, we must look to the Holy Word and to the revealed science of correspondences for it. In the first place we know, by the general law, that as God is Love and Wisdom; and that Love and Wisdom are composed of goods and truths in infinite variety, forming a perfect whole; and as all natural things were created by, or sprang from that infinite goodness and truth, so each natural thing must correspond to some truth or some good either in true or in inverted order. And as we further know, that purging or cleansing of the mind, must be done by truths; we may therefore see that as hyssop is always used in the Word for cleansing, it must denote natural truth in its cleansing properties. For the various loves of self, from which we are to be purified, cannot be known but by the light of natural truth, and therefore cannot be otherwise removed. For truths cannot be used for cleansing until they are known: because cleansing is a work which cannot be done in the dark. We may therefore see, from the general light before us, that to purge with hyssop must mean to cleanse with truths. Therefore hyssop is always used, wherever it occurs in the Word, for cleansing.

Cedar wood and hyssop are sometimes mentioned in connection, for cleansing, where cedar means internal or spiritual truths, and hyssop external or natural truths. That hyssop denotes lower truth and cedar higher, is evident from 1 Kings iv. 33, where it speaks of

" trees, from the cedar tree that is in Lebanon even unto the hyssop that springeth out of the wall :" thus embracing the whole range of truths, from spiritual to natural.

Trees in general, in a good sense, signify the members of the church, or the church in them, as to intelligence from its doctrines, and from the truths of the Word. Sometimes they denote the good desires men feel, and the works they perform. In a bad sense, they signify the opposites of these.

The natural forest has long been admired as an emblem of the human family. For in the woods, as among men, are all ages, from the great-great-grandfather down to infancy ; and the prior generations lie scattered on the ground. We behold the beautiful tree and the ugly, the wholesome and the poisonous, the perfect and the injured, the fruitful and the barren, the free and the cross-grained, the smooth and the thorny, the crookèd and the straight, the healthy and the sick, the living and the dead ; the black, white, red, brown and yellow ; some dying of good old age, others swept away by the tornado in the bloom of youth, and others crushed in infancy and childhood. Thus the forest, in a natural point of view, is a beautiful emblem of the human family.

But the scene becomes doubly interesting and important when we perceive that there is a perfect and eternal law of analogy between mankind and the trees, both cultivated and uncultivated. When we understand that the varieties and qualities of the trees are the result of the varieties and qualities of the spiritual states, principles and propensities of men; and that all that is said of them, in the Word, is symbolically expressive of the qualities of men's hearts and minds; and that in these familiar symbols, we may learn human nature, and the will of our heavenly Father, and the way of eternal life, and behold the invisible things of God from the creation of the world:—I say, When we understand this, we are prepared to say with the Psalmist, "The trees of the LORD are full of sap; the cedars of Lebanon, which He hath planted." "Praise ye Him, sun and moon: praise Him, all ye stars of light." "Mountains, and all hills; fruitful trees, and all cedars: beasts, and all cattle. . . . Praise ye the LORD." For in saying this we are only calling upon *man* to praise the Lord with all the principles and elements of his nature, to which these natural things correspond.

In Judges, we have this singular parable. "The trees went forth to anoint a king over them; and they said unto the olive-tree, Reign thou over us. But the olive-tree said unto them, Should I leave my fatness, wherewith by me they honor God and man, and go to be promoted over the trees? And the trees said to the fig-tree, Come thou, and reign over us. But the fig-tree said unto them, Should I forsake my sweetness, and my good fruit, and go to be promoted over the trees? Then said the trees unto the vine, Come thou, and reign over us. And the vine said unto them, Should I leave my wine, which cheereth God and man, and go to be promoted over the trees? Then said all the trees unto the bramble, Come thou, and reign over us. And the bramble said unto the trees, If in truth ye anoint me king over you, then come and put your trust in my shadow: and if not, let fire come out of the bramble, and devour the cedars of Lebanon." (ix. 8–15.)

Before the spiritual sense of this parable can be known, it must be understood what is meant by the olive-tree, the fig-tree, the vine, and the bramble. The olive-tree here signifies celestial good; the vine, spiritual good; the fig-tree, natural good; and the bramble, spurious good. By celestial good we mean that principle or state of heart which loves God or goodness supremely: by spiritual good, that state which loves the Word or truth supremely: and by natural good, that state which loves kind words or use supremely: but by spurious good, we mean a perverted state of heart, which loves evil and self supremely.

The trees, in this parable, denote the people of the kingdom of Israel, in that age, who had become so corrupt that they would not be ruled by the Lord. They also denote any people of any age who are thus corrupt. By the refusal of the olive-tree to reign over them, we learn that they were too low to be governed by internal or celestial goodness, or by love to God. For the olive-tree says, Should I leave my fatness, wherewith by me they honor God and man? This fatness denotes the good of celestial love, or love to God. Therefore to be their king, the olive-tree would have to leave his fatness before the trees would promote him. For when the olive-tree replied to their call, saying, Shall I leave my fatness, wherewith they honor God and man, and go to be promoted over the trees? they made no reply, but turned to the fig-tree. Gladly would the olive-tree have reigned over them, had they yielded to his goodness.

By the refusal of the fig-tree, we learn that they were too depraved to submit to the government of even external or natural good springing from the love of obedience. For the fig-tree says, Should I forsake my sweetness, and my good fruit? And what is more sweet than natural kindness and mercy carried out in good works or fruits? The people were not willing to come under the laws of good works and do as they would be done by. And they would not promote the fig-tree, unless he would forsake these heavenly principles, and give them laws more in accordance with their self-love.

By the refusal of the vine, we learn that they would not be governed by spiritual goodness, springing from the love of truth. For the vine said, Should I leave my wine, which cheereth God and man? They were not willing to love the truth, and be governed by that love: and therefore, they would not promote the vine, unless he would throw off that restraint from his government.

But, by their consenting to be governed by the bramble, they show that they were in the love of perverted goodness; of hypocrisy and selfhood; and so they chose that these principles of their nature, represented by the bramble, should govern their conduct. They were willing to put themselves under the darkening shadow of their own licentiousness—the vile bramble of self-love. And here they expected to be satisfied and happy. But as predicted, fire came out of the bramble and devoured the cedars of Lebanon ; or, in other words, the lusts of evil and self-love destroyed in them all the remaining principles of truth and good.

This parable, though particularly applicable to the age in which it was written, comes, with its blessed instruction, like all other portions of the divine Word, to every individual of depraved humanity in all ages ; and it proposes to him the solemn question, By what are you governed ? the olive, the fig, the vine, or the bramble ? And how shall we individually answer ? Who can say he is governed by the olive—the pure love of interior goodness ? To whom of us does not the olive-tree say, Should I leave my fatness to be promoted over you ? Or who is willing to submit to the pure government of the olive ? None of us is ready to say he is governed by that pure love. And who of us can say he has the vine for a governor ? Who feels that he is governed, in his conduct, by the pure love of the truth ? To whom does not the vine say, Should I leave my wine—my heavenly truth—and come down to your state and receive your selfish promotion ? Yes, we ask, who is entirely ready to fully submit to the government of spiritual truth ? I know of none that would say I, to this question. And who can even say he is governed by the fig-tree—the full love of natural goodness—whereby he obediently and affectionately keeps the commandments of his divine Master ? It is a great deal to be in so good a state as not to have the fig-tree say, Should I forsake my sweetness, and my good fruit, in order to gain your approbation and receive your vote to become your king ? I do not know who considers himself fully governed by the fig-tree.

Sad, then, indeed is the spiritual state of mankind, even in this age of freedom and science. The most that the best are willing to say is, that they hope they are, to some extent, governed by these heavenly principles of the Lord ; and that they are praying and striving, by the powers of the blessed Spirit, to become wholly released from the brambles of self-love.

But the question is asked, How are we to know that the olive, vine and fig-tree mean what is here stated ? Are we to take a man's word for it ? We answer, No : God's Word clearly teaches it. In the first place, with these significations of these trees, we have rational instruction, from the parable explained, and receive from it useful rules of life. But, without the spiritual meaning, it teaches us nothing. Here is at once an evidence of its truth.

The olive-tree signifies celestial good, from the quality of the tree. It is a tree of oil. Oil denotes this goodness. Oil burns, and its fire denotes love. So celestial goodness burns with heavenly love, to the Lord. It is for this reason that it is said, in prophecy, through Jeremiah, of the church, when in order, "The LORD called thy name, A green olive-tree, fair, and of goodly fruit." Now, for a church or an individual to be a green olive-tree, fair, and of goodly fruit, is to be alive in love to the Lord, bearing the fruits of kindness and love to the neighbor. That olive-trees mean celestial principles of the mind, or men of those principles, is evident from the condition in which olive-trees were seen in the spiritual world. For nothing exists or is seen in the spiritual world, but principles of the mind and the persons from whom those principles are manifest; for that is a world of mind.

Zechariah saw two olive-trees in the spiritual world. They were called the two anointed ones that stand by the Lord of the whole earth. They were seen standing by two golden candlesticks. And they are called the two witnesses. And the candlesticks are also called the two witnesses. Now, that these candlesticks and olive-trees denote principles of the mind, we may know, by their being called the two witnesses. Saint John saw these witnesses, and says, "These are the two olive-trees, and the two candlesticks standing before the God of the earth." These two witnesses are love to God and the neighbor. They signify man's heavenly state of mind. These principles are the witnesses, or evidences of our preparation for heaven. And they who possess them are called olive-trees. Thus, David, who represented the Lord, says, "I am like a green olive-tree in the house of my God."

That the vine denotes, in this parable, spiritual goodness, or spiritual truth loved, is abundantly evident from the Word; indeed we could cite a volume. The Lord, as to His spiritual principle, as the Word, which is the truth, says, "I am the vine." And the fact that wine corresponds to spiritual truth, is evidence enough.

And that the fig-tree corresponds to natural good, may be seen from the fact that often when natural goodness and truth are described in the Word by works, use is made of the fig-tree, or of figs, or fig-leaves ; as in Jeremiah, when the people did not bring forth the fruits of external faith and obedience ; the prophet says, "There shall be no . . . . figs on the fig-tree, and the leaf shall fade." But when the people bring forth the fruits of kindness, in good works, it is written in Joel, "The fig-tree yields its strength." A judgment was executed upon the fig-tree, because it did not bear fruit. This was to teach man that he must do the works—the external things. And the Lord says to that fig-tree, "No man eat fruit of thee hereafter for ever." "And presently the fig-tree withered away." It was because the fig-tree denotes works of kindness and mercy that it was selected by the Lord to teach this lesson. And though a judgment was passed upon the barren fig-tree, yet it was spiritually passed upon the unfruitful man.

The principles represented in this parable, by the fig, the vine and the olive, which are the natural, the spiritual and the celestial, are often mentioned together in the Holy Word ; the same as corn, wine and oil, which represent the same things. They point to the three great essential principles in God—power, wisdom and love. In man, they are use, truth and goodness ; or works, faith and charity, symbolized in the parable by the fig, the vine and the olive. And they are brought up in the parable to teach us that unless we are governed by some one of these principles, we shall be lost—destroyed by the fire of the bramble, or of self-love.

In the celestial heavens, the angels are governed by

the olive-tree, or by celestial good, which is the love of good.

In the spiritual heavens, they are governed by the vine, or by spiritual good, which is the love of truth.

In the natural heavens, they are governed by the fig-tree, or by natural good, which is the love of use, or of good works.

Therefore, to be governed by either of these loves, will give us heaven—the love of good, the love of truth, or the love of use. But if not willing to be governed by either, the vile bramble must take us.

That trees denote *persons* as well as principles, may be known by any one who will carefully and candidly examine the thirty-first chapter of Ezekiel. For there, Pharaoh is called the Assyrian, and also a cedar of Lebanon. And this cedar had grown so great, shot up its top so high, and spread out its branches so wide, that "all the fowls of heaven made their nests in his boughs, and under his branches did all the beasts of the field bring forth their young, and under his shadow dwelt all great nations." He became so great, that "all the trees of Eden, that were in the garden of God, envied him." "The fir-trees were not like his boughs, and the chestnut-trees were not like his branches;" and even "the cedars in the garden of God could not hide him." But, from the height of this glory he fell. And at his fall, "all the trees of the field fainted." And it is declared by the Lord that all the trees of Eden, the choicest and best of Lebanon, shall be comforted in the nether parts of the earth: And that they also went down into hell with him. And when they went down the Lord says, "I covered the deep for him, and I restrained the floods thereof, and the great waters were stayed."

Now, although it is at once obvious, by this chapter, that trees signify persons or principles in them, and although the last sentence in the chapter declares that this is Pharaoh and all his multitude ; yet, to simply know this and no more, is of but little use. The essential teachings cannot be known without the science of correspondences. For, how is a man to know, from mere fanciful tropes and figures of speech, what these things mean ? He cannot thus know them. But the Most High God speaks not in so weak and uncertain a language as metaphor. His speech is eternal and unchangeable, definite and sure, carrying in its bosom spirit and life. It is yea and amen ; positive and certain : and so plain that he who runs may read. But if we would truly read, we must *run* : and the race must be heavenward.

We have not space to give the spiritual signification of this chapter, but will glance at some of its leading features. Pharaoh king of Egypt represents the natural man in the love of science ; and progressing in scientific wisdom and knowledge, and thereby gaining great power and influence, becoming envied and admired for his vast acquirements and superior excellence, until he becomes great in his own estimation, inflated with self-love, and thus he falls into ruinous evils. The various conditions of the trees and birds and beasts, and the waters, show the operations of the various principles of his mind to which these natural things correspond as he rises to the zenith of his glory and falls into darkness and death. And in the sure language of God, we may find it exceedingly interesting and instructive, as applicable to our natural man by the rules of analogy. And these correspondences may be abundantly sustained from the Word; for they are among the most common symbols, and always mean preeisely the same things when used in the same relations.

And what a beautiful history this parable gives of the scientific development of the human mind: and then of its becoming proud of its own wisdom, forgetful of its God as the fountain of knowledge, and thus wise in its own eyes, until it falls into spiritual death! And what a warning to us, lest we become inflated with self-importance in consequence of the wisdom we see in this heavenly light; and thus imagine ourselves good and wise above our neighbors, until we lose the pure, interior light in the false glare of self-derived intelligence!

But to our text. "The thistle that was in Lebanon sent to the cedar that was in Lebanon, saying, Give thy daughter to my son to wife." From what has been said, all must be ready to look into the mind for the thistle and the cedar. And while the cedar denotes the spiritual man, or high interior truths, the thistle denotes a low, external, vicious principle. As natural thistles choke the good seeds of earth and prevent their growth, so they correspond to those falsities of the mind which prevent the divine seed of the Word from taking root in the heart.

Hosea, prophesying of the fallen state of the church

says, "The thorn and the thistle shall come up on their altars." Now, the true altar where the real incense is offered to God is the grateful and contrite heart. Wicked hearts are therefore the altars to which the prophet here alludes. For natural thistles grow not upon the altars of churches.

"The thistle that was in Lebanon." Lebanon is a mountain in Palestine. In the Word, a mountain denotes a high state of the mind, either for good or for evil. The thistle here denotes a false and vile principle, and the cedar a true and virtuous one. And both of these principles may be in the same mind, or may not. The will is the female element of the mind, and the understanding is the male element. The daughter of the cedar, therefore, is a young and noble principle of the will; and the son of the thistle is a young and vicious principle of the understanding. Thus, as regards the same mind; the thistle or a falsity in the male department of the mind is asking for a union with the cedar or with a virtue, in the female department. Or in other words; some falsity in the understanding is seeking a marriage with some good in the will. Now, vicious principles of the mind are always striving to bring down to their level the virtuous principles; to unite the cedar with the thistle.

But we have not only the thistle and the cedar in the same mind; but we have the thistles and cedars of society. Where the thistle principle in a man rules, he may be called a thistle; where the cedar principle rules, he may be called a cedar. And let the young men, the noble young cedars of the community beware, lest they be led astray by the thistles that stroll in our streets, and which lure to the dens of intemperance and vice. For if they once fall into the embrace of the thistle, they will be in danger of coming to the same end as the thistle in the text ; which is deplorable enough. For the words following our text declare, that " there passed by a wild beast that was in Lebanon, and trode down the thistle ;" thus showing that such principles are low as the dust, and are under the very feet of the wild and unsubdued passions of the perverted will ; trodden under the feet of wild beasts.

But in these latter days the Lord is mercifully providing us with a safeguard against all these evils by opening to us the deeper truths of His Word whereby we may scan ourselves to the bottom, understand the causes and consequences of transgression, and see the way of escape from every vice. Then let us receive the Holy Word to our bosoms, seek its divine light, yield to its divine power, and thus ascend Mount Lebanon to its summit, where we can stand among its heavenly cedars and hold familiar converse with the lovely trees of Eden in the paradise of God.

CHAPTER VIII.

SYMBOLIC MEANING OF HEAVENS AND EARTH, SUN, MOON AND STARS.

"The sun shall be darkened, and the moon shall not give her light, and the stars shall fall from heaven, and the powers of the heavens shall be shaken." (Matt. xxiv. 29.)

HERE are divine ideas contained in human language —the mere words of men. But there is a divine speech within, the idiom of which is analogical. This analogy enables us to perceive something of the divine idea in and through the human speech. This analogy exists in and throughout nature. There we are to look for it, there we are to study it as the law of life. It is that law which connects the creation with the Creator. And by it we are to look through the visible universe into the mind of the Creator, and also into the minds of men, the images of God. God's language therefore is not an empty sign of ideas, but a living sign, expressive of the laws of life. It is neither Hebrew nor Greek, nor any other human language. But as all human dialects are taken from nature, and as God fills nature, so he speaks in any one of the human languages, when the words are so selected and arranged as to contain divine ideas by correspondences. God's language therefore is substantial life; the very life which exists throughout nature and speaks through it: for He says, "The words which I speak unto you, they are spirit and they are life." Thus the things of nature are all letters and syllables, words and sentences, spoken by ten thousand tongues, all in action from the living universal speech of God. Our heavenly Father therefore, in order to speak to His children and teach them the nature of Himself and the laws of life, by written words, had to come down to man's own language, and thus clothe His divine speech in the common, finite words of the people. This was the only way He could reach our capacities. But, by His divine influence, He enabled the writers of His Word, to so select the words and frame the sentences as to contain, by correspondences, a spiritual or divine sense, which can be seen only by the divine law of analogy.

Thus God speaks to us, in man's own language, in the literal sense; and, at the same time, in the divine speech in the spiritual sense. But in reading the Word, some see only man's language. Yet, as it is divinely arranged and infilled with life by correspondences, even the literal sense contains a power which is felt in no other human composition. And if men humbly receive it and obey its literal commands, it will surely take them to heaven; because, from its internal powers it will make them heavenly. Why then, it may be asked, is any further sense necessary? We answer, because the true literal sense has, in many of its doctrines, been falsified by the traditions of men; and the scientific world is passing it by as not a divine work. The time, therefore, has arrived for the Lord to appear as the spirit and life of that Book, that He may therein reach, anew, the souls of men, through their rational faculties ; expressing at the same time, the truth of the letter and the power and glory of the Spirit. While, therefore, some persons see in the Bible only the language of men, others see therein, the language of God.

But the divine speech, is the great language—the universal speech—the one in which the heavens and the earth are conversing together—the one which we shall all speak in the spiritual world. And because of the high importance of the spiritual sense of the Holy Word, the literal sense in many places, is given only for the sake of the spiritual. And in these instances the letter is often totally dark and incomprehensible, until the spiritual sense is seen. Such is the case with our text. The letter alone is total darkness. Science looks it in the face and exclaims, What ! The stars fall from heaven to this earth ! And what are the stars but vast suns to other systems ? And, which way is down from those great centres ? And what, in comparison, is this little planet upon which we live, but a mere atom of dust ? How is *it* to draw the universe to its comparative nothingness ? And where would it and its inhabitants be, if it were in the centre of the whole immense mass of all matter, in one solid body ? And how could the Lord then come to us in the clouds of heaven ? For, following our text, and after the stars have fallen the narrative says, "And then shall all the tribes of the earth mourn, and they shall see the Son of man coming in the clouds of heaven with power and great glory." Let us then seek the spiritual import of our text, and, thereby a true knowledge of the subject before us.

Our full theme is, The symbolic meaning of the heavens and the earth, the sun, moon and stars, as understood in the divine language. And as the human mind is a microcosm, or world in miniature, and the universe of things corresponds to it, so the phrase, *the heavens and the earth,* means the human mind.—The heavens, the internal mind or the spiritual man; and the earth, the external mind, or natural man. In the internal plane of the mind, we hold communion with our God, and with heavenly things. In the external plane, we have intercourse with men, and with earthly things. We feel conscious of an elevation of mind above natural things, when we enter into our closet, in devotional meditations. And there, through the Word, we receive light from the Sun of righteousness; or the divine truth comes to illumine, warm and fructify our earth or natural mind, that it may bring forth the fruits of good works; the same correspondentially as the natural earth receives light and warmth from the sun of the natural heavens, that it may yield its fruits.

Now, the Holy Word commences by saying, "In the beginning God created the heavens and the earth. And the earth was without form, and void." And the order which follows, in the chapter, shows, by analogy, the process of the creation of this mental heaven and earth, or of man, until we see him in the full human form, in the image and likeness of his God. Now this image and likeness is what makes man to be the church; for the image is the divine truth, and the likeness is the divine good, in man; and these constitute the kingdom of God in the human mind. And because by analogy the divine phrase, "The heavens and the earth," means the human mind and not the natural universe, therefore, an account of the creation of the heaven and the earth, or of the human mind, is not confined to the first chapter of Genesis.

The Lord says in Isaiah, "Behold, I create new heavens and a new earth: and the former shall not be remembered, nor come into mind." Now what is meant by the former heavens and earth, which are not to be remembered, unless it be the very heavens and earth which the same Bible mentions as having been created in the beginning? It is positively certain that the Lord means, by the new heavens and new earth, here mentioned, a new state of the human mind; or man again restored to the image and likeness of God; having his external mind or earth in God's image, and his internal mind or heavens in God's likeness; for the prophecy continues, "Behold, I create Jerusalem a rejoicing, and her people a joy." And Jerusalem, all may see, means the church or the human mind in order. Now, this prophecy in Isaiah, relates to the coming of the Lord in the flesh, for the establishment of the Christian church, or of a new state of the human mind. And this state of the mind is the new heavens and the new earth to which the prophecy refers. For the former heavens and earth, or good and true state of mind, had passed away in the progressive fall of man, wherein the image and likeness of God were lost; and the new heavens and earth were to take their place.

In the prophecy through Jeremiah our Lord says, in reference to this dark state of the human mind or of the church, "My people is foolish, they have not known me; they are sottish children, and they have none understanding: they are wise to do evil, but to do good they have no knowledge. I beheld the earth, and, lo, it was without form and void; and the heavens, and they had no light. I beheld, and, lo, there was no man, and all the birds of the heavens were fled." (iv. 22, 23, 25.) Here, we have the state of a depraved mind, or of a consummated church. For it is to the condition of the Jewish church or people, at the time the Lord was to come in the flesh, that this prophecy relates. And how much it is like the description of the state of the first people on earth, while in spiritual ignorance, before the kingdom of heaven was established in them. For that narrative, in Genesis, says, "In the beginning God created the heaven and the earth. And the earth was without form, and void; and darkness was upon the face of the deep." And the prophecy in Jeremiah says, "I beheld the earth, and, lo, it was without form and void; the heavens, and they had no light. I beheld, and, lo, there was no man." Can we, then, come to any other conclusion than that it was the state of the human mind that was meant in both instances? In the first instance the minds of the first people were undeveloped, and therefore in mental darkness; their mental earth was void of light and knowledge, and therefore, formless as to true beauty; but the Lord went on afterward and progressively created them in His own image.

In the prophecy in Jeremiah, the Jewish mind at the coming of the Lord, was without form and void, because it was not symmetrical, being deformed by sin, and void of goodness and truth. Its heavens or internal mind, as the prophecy declares, had no light, for they had ceased to be spiritual. And the reason it is said, *I beheld, and, lo, there was no man,* is, it requires the image and likeness of God to make a real man; and these they had lost. And so, the reason it is said that all the birds of heaven had fled is, all heavenly thoughts were gone. The Jews had become a low, sensual people. The natural earth was not void nor formless. It rolled, as usual, "along its airy way" and produced its fruits; while the heavenly bodies still sent forth their cheering light, and the merry birds warbled as ever their melodious notes. But the mental earth of the people was without form and void, their heavens had no light and the heavenly birds were fled, and there was no real man left—nothing truly manly.

Now, what would have to be done, in order to restore to man the image and likeness of God? What, but to re-animate the mental earth with new affections, set the lights of truth again in the heavens, to give light upon the earth; call back the fled birds, or heavenly thoughts, and thus give to the mind its true form and comeliness? And all this the Lord did in the establishment of the Christian church. He created man again in His own image and likeness.—Or He created a new heavens and a new earth, or His church in man, and illuminated it. And He says to it, prophetically, "Arise, shine; for thy light is come, and the glory of the LORD is risen upon thee; and the Gentiles shall come to thy light, and kings to the brightness of thy rising." Isa. lx. 1, 3.

Thus the Lord is the light of the mind or of the church. The sun denotes the Lord as to love and wisdom; the moon denotes truth or faith; and the stars, truths or knowledges. They are never mentioned in the Word without having this signification.

The sun is the most striking symbol of the Lord in all nature. By its heat and light it performs the same use to the natural earth which the Lord, by His love and wisdom, does to the mental earth or human mind. And the analogy is perfect, and is everywhere maintained throughout the Holy Word. And as the sun represents the Lord in the Word, so the earth and sky represent the human mind. And as the natural earth without the sun, with its heat and light, is cold and dark, so a human mind without the Lord, with His love and wisdom, is cold and dark. And as clouds in the atmosphere darken the earth, by shutting out the light of the sun, so clouds of ignorance and error, in the understanding, darken the mind and shut out the light and truth coming from the Lord, the Sun of Righteousness. And as, after a season of clouds and storms and darkness, the light of the sun makes its appearance through the clouds of the natural heavens, illuminating and rejoicing the earth; so the Lord, as the Light of the Sun of Righteousness, after an age of error and warfare and darkness with the children of men, comes in the clouds of the human mind or mental heavens, to enlighten and rejoice the souls of men and establish His kingdom again among them.

And as the sun is used in the Word, as a symbol of the Lord as to the Divine Love and Wisdom, so the moon is used as a symbol of man's faith. For as the moon is a dark, opaque body, receiving all its light from the sun, so the human mind is a dark body receiving all its light of truth or its true faith, from the Lord, the Sun of Righteousness. We have no real faith but as the Lord gives it to us by the Light of His Truth: and so the moon has no light but as the sun gives it from the glory of its beams. And as the human mind shines by the truths of faith from the Lord, so the moon shines by light borrowed from the sun. The moon is therefore used in the Word as a true symbol of faith.

And the stars are most beautiful symbols of truths or knowledges in the mind. Being bright objects in the natural firmament, they denote true principles in the understanding or mental firmament. What a beautiful mental constellation are the ten commandments when bright and clear in the firmament of the mind! Like beacon lights to the natural mariner, they stand in our mental heavens as fixed stars, upon which we may ever depend to mark our moral and religious latitude and longitude in the ocean of life, as we strive, in dependence upon the Lord, to guide our frail bark of humanity on its onward-bound voyage to the haven of peace—our eternal home. Stars are therefore always used in the Word as symbols of truths or of knowledges in the human mind: and with this signification the Word is made plain where stars are used.

Stars are therefore said to fall from heaven or to withdraw their shining, whenever man loses his knowledges of the truths of the Word. Therefore, in the prophecy in Joel of the end of the church, the Lord says, "The earth shall quake; the heavens shall tremble: the sun and the moon shall be dark, and the stars shall withdraw their shining: the sun shall be turned into darkness, and the moon into blood." (ii. 10, 31.) This is a prophetic description of the dark and troubled state of the human mind when its sun of Righteousness, its moon of faith, and its stars of spiritual knowledge, cease to shine.

And how graphic is this description when the analogy is seen! No human language can compare with it, either for fulness, definiteness, or force. What a pitiable state of man, or of the mental earth, is shown by the following language through Isaiah! "The earth mourneth and fadeth away. The earth is defiled. The foundations of the earth do shake. The earth is utterly broken down. The earth is clean dissolved. The earth is moved exceedingly. The earth shall reel to and fro like a drunkard." (xxiv. 4, 5, 18, 19, 20.) If the earth here means the church, or a dark and troubled state of mind, all is rational. But if it does not mean the mind, what does it mean?

If the Lord created a new heavens and a new earth at His first coming, as the Holy Word declares, and that heavens and earth do not mean the church, or a good state of the human mind, what do they mean? As these things did not happen to the sun, moon and stars, at the Lord's coming, when the prophecy was fulfilled, they must signify something else. And we have positive testimony in the Scriptures, in plain and unmistakable language, that they do mean something else, and also, what they mean.

On the day of pentecost, when the people were all amazed, and marvelled, saying one to another, "Are not all these who speak Galileans? and how hear we every man in our own tongue, wherein we were born? Parthians, and Medes, and Elamites, and the dwellers in Mesopotamia, and in Judea, and Cappadocia, in Pontus, and Asia, Phrygia, and Pamphylia, in Egypt, and in the parts of Lybia about Cyrene, and strangers of Rome, Jews and proselytes, Cretes and Arabians, we do hear them speak in our tongues the wonderful works of God. But Peter, standing up with the eleven, lifted up his voice, and said unto them, Ye men of Judea, and all ye that dwell at Jerusalem, be this known unto you, and hearken to my words: This is that which was spoken by the prophet Joel; And it shall come to pass in the last days, saith God, I will pour out of my spirit upon all flesh: and your sons and your daughters shall prophesy, and your young men shall see visions, and your old men shall dream dreams: and on my servants and on my handmaidens I will pour out, in those days, of my spirit, and they shall prophesy: and I will show wonders in heaven above, and signs in the earth beneath; blood, and fire, and vapor of smoke:

The sun shall be turned into darkness, and the moon into blood, before that great and notable day of the Lord come : and it shall come to pass, that whoever shall call upon the name of the Lord shall be saved." (Acts ii. 7–21.) Here Peter quotes the very words of Joel, who declares that, before the things mentioned as occurring on the day of pentecost should take place, the sun should be turned into darkness and the moon into blood : thus showing clearly that before the Christian church should be established, there would be no true light of faith in the human mind on earth. For by the sun's being turned into darkness, is meant the loss of all true knowledge and love of the Lord, the Sun of Righteousness. And by the moon's being turned into blood is meant, violence done to faith.

There can be no question of the meaning of these prophecies left in the mind of any one who will candidly examine them in that light of analogy in which they are written.

The same symbolic language is used, in the prophetic portions of the New Testament, to express another dark, divided and distracted state of the religious world on the earth, and of the establishment of the New Jerusalem. And it is used in too plain a manner to be mistaken by any unprejudiced and humble seeker after truth, who will examine the science of correspondences : For the prophet John says, in the Apocalypse, " And I saw a new heaven and a new earth ; for the first heaven and the first earth were passed away ; and I John saw the holy city, new Jerusalem, coming down from God out of heaven, prepared as a bride adorned for her husband. And I heard a great voice out of heaven, saying, Behold, the tabernacle of God is with men, and He will dwell with them, and they shall be His people, and God Himself shall be with them, their God." (Rev. xxi. 1, 2, 3.)

Now, in taking a candid and rational view of the whole Word on this subject, we ask the serious mind if the new heavens and the new earth mentioned in this prophecy of St. John can, consistently with the rest of the divine Word, be possibly construed to mean anything else than a new church, or a new state of religious life? As it is beyond dispute certain that the Lord came the first time to supercede the Jewish church by a higher order of faith and life, and that He established it by a new heavens and a new earth in the minds of His disciples: why then, we ask, is it not a still higher order of faith and life that the Lord comes to establish by the creation of another new heavens and new earth in advance of those created at His first coming, and wherein all shall see eye to eye? Can any one doubt from the tenor of the whole quotation from St. John, that the new heavens and new earth, which he saw, mean a new church? The question then is plainly settled, from the Holy Word, that the phrase "the heavens and the earth" means the church, or the human mind in order.

Now, the whole 24th chapter of Matthew is a prophecy of the divisions, disorders and troubles which would arise in the Christian world, and of the coming of the Lord for the establishment of the New Jerusalem. And in that portion from which our text is taken the

Lord says, "Immediately after the tribulation of those days shall the sun be darkened, and the moon shall not give her light, and the stars shall fall from heaven, and the powers of the heavens shall be shaken: and then shall appear the sign of the Son of man in heaven: and then shall all the tribes of the earth mourn; and they shall see the Son of man coming in the clouds of heaven with power and great glory." All these wonderful things of the sun, moon and stars were to take place before the coming of the Lord in the clouds of heaven and the descent of the New Jerusalem.

Now, as the things prophesied of the sun, moon and stars did not take place in outward nature at the Lord's first coming, as prophesied in Isaiah, Jeremiah and Joel, we therefore are not to look for anything of the kind at his second coming; for it is declared, in both instances, that the same things would take place.

How can the natural stars—vast suns to other systems—fall to this little earth? But if the stars mean knowledges of truth, they might fall from the mental heavens. The understanding might become so darkened by sin as not to see nor regard the truths of the Word at all. I know it is believed by many pious Christians, that this prophecy, in Matthew, is to be literally fulfilled in that the Lord will personally come, in the natural clouds which float in our atmosphere. But where would the clouds be after the stars had fallen? For He is not to appear until after the stars have fallen, and the sun has been darkened. And how is the Son of man to be seen in those clouds without any light? Besides, if the stars should fall to the earth, we should have all the material bodies of the vast universe collected in one mass and this little earth in the very centre.

But the doctrine of the falling of the stars is now generally given up, among civilized people. It was once supposed to be true: but since the science of astronomy has revealed some of the laws which govern the heavenly bodies, and something of their distances and magnitudes, thinking people no longer believe that the stars will fall. But in giving up the falling of the stars, many give up the Bible also, disbelieving it to be divine wisdom; for they think it plainly teaches that the stars do fall. And many good people of the various Christian denominations, who still adhere to the divinity of the Word, and acknowledge the falling of the stars to be figurative language, continue to believe that the Lord will make His second coming in a personal form, in the visible clouds. But, upon what grounds of Scripture interpretation can any one come to the conclusion that that entire quotation from Matthew, all in one sentence, should be figurative language, except the coming of the Lord in the clouds, and that *that* part should be literal, as it reads?

But all will be plain when men see that the clouds are the dark literal sense of the Word, when not understood; and that the Lord, who is the Word itself in its spirit and life, will make His coming, as the spiritual light of the Word, in those clouds, by means of the science of correspondences. Who does not see that, without that science, the letter of our text is a dark cloud in the mind? But by the use of that science the Lord, as heavenly light, comes in this cloud with power and great glory.

The passage in Mark, which treats of the second coming of the Lord, and of the state of the Christian world, reads thus, " But in those days, after the tribulation, the sun shall be darkened, and the moon shall not give her light, and the stars of heaven shall fall." By " the tribulation of those days " is meant, what we now see in the Christian world, as divisions and subdivisions, and contentions of sects and parties and creeds, called, in the prophetic teachings of the 24th chapter of Matthew, " wars and rumors of wars, and famines, and pestilences, and earthquakes ;" and cryings, " Lo, here is Christ, or there." But in Isaiah (lx. 18, 20), where the coming of the New Jerusalem is predicted, our Lord says, " Violence shall no more be heard in thy land, wasting nor destruction within thy borders; but thou shalt call thy walls Salvation, and thy gates Praise. Thy sun shall no more go down ; neither shall thy moon withdraw itself : for the LORD shall be thine everlasting light, and the days of thy mourning shall be ended." Thus showing, that the New Jerusalem is to be the crowning and final church, and is to have no end : that its sun and moon will always shine : for, says the Word, " The glory of God did lighten it, and the Lamb is the light thereof." The Sun of Righteousness is its Sun.

In one of the prophecies of the New Jerusalem through St. John, it says, " There appeared a great wonder in heaven ; a woman clothed with the Sun, and the moon under her feet, and upon her head a crown of twelve stars." This woman denotes the crowning church. She is to come as a bride adorned for her husband. And how sumptuous may become her embellishments when she has, by analogy, such free access to the divine rubies, and pearls, and gems of the Holy Word, of every heavenly variety and beauty! Now, with the signification which analogy gives to the sun, moon and stars, this prophecy is most rational and beautiful. While, without that signification, it teaches us nothing. How cheering the thought that the church is yet to be clothed with light as with a garment—a light shining from heavenly love—so that her deportment will be pure mercy and intelligence: that her understanding is to be filled with all spiritual knowledges, symbolized by a crown of twelve stars: that she will ever stand firm upon the eternal rock of true faith, denoted by the moon under her feet, as a sure lantern to her paths!

There is another striking prophecy in the Apocalypse, concerning the disturbed and beclouded condition of the Christian world preceding the descent of the New Jerusalem. It reads thus:—"The sun became black as sackcloth of hair, and the moon became as blood; and the stars of heaven fell unto the earth, even as a fig-tree casteth her untimely figs, when she is shaken of a mighty wind: and the heaven departed as a scroll when it is rolled together." (Rev. vi. 12–14.) Here again, the literal sense is utterly incomprehensible. We cannot conceive of stars falling from heaven as blighted figs, blown off by the wind. But we can conceive of truths, by a wicked life, becoming apparently blighted, withered away, and lost to the human mind. Nor can we conceive of the moon's becoming blood. But we can conceive of violence done to a true faith, until it is crimsoned with sins of every dye.

Now, we have given a brief explanation of the meaning of the heavens and the earth; the sun, moon and stars, from the very commencement of the Word to its close.—In Genesis, in the prophets, in the gospels, the Acts of the Apostles, as taken from the prophets, and in Revelation. The literal sense alone is against the reason which God has given to man, and consequently cannot teach him. We may safely say this, because it has not been able to teach him. It has baffled the skill of the most learned and pious commentators. They have all differed in their opinions; and have honestly declared themselves ignorant of the meaning intended to be conveyed.

But by the divine science of correspondences, in which the Holy Word is written, we have a rational and beautiful view of the truths therein taught. And what is most important is, they show us our God and teach us the way of life and salvation; the very things which we most need to know, and which the good God most desires to teach us. "O that men would praise the Lord for His goodness, and for His wonderful works to the children of men; for He satisfieth the longing soul, and filleth the hungry soul with goodness." Ps. cvii. 8, 9.

CHAPTER IX.

THE FIRST CHAPTER OF GENESIS IN ITS SPIRITUAL IMPORT—THE CREATION OF MAN.

"And God said, Let us make man in our image, after our likeness." (Gen. i. 26.)

In this lecture we propose to treat upon the first chapter of Genesis, in its spiritual import—the creation of man. This chapter has generally been looked upon as a history of the creation of the material universe. For, after the loss of the science of correspondences, and while men remained ignorant of the lower sciences, and particularly of Astronomy, Geology, and Chemistry, they were in much mental darkness as to the physical laws as well as the spiritual. And in this ignorance, the literal sense of the account of the creation, was adapted to their gross states and wants. It was good for them to read it, to reverence it, and to believe it. For thereby they acknowledged the Lord, in His infinity, as the creator and sustainer of the universe. And they could therein regard Him as their heavenly Father. This instruction was just what they needed. It was all their states could bear.

But men were not always to remain in this ignorance. They were made for higher light and life than nature gives. But before they could advance to spiritual knowledge, they must lay its foundation in nature. It was for this reason that their existence commenced in this material mode of life. "First that which is natural, and afterward that which is spiritual."

And as men investigated nature and reasoned upon her laws, the natural sciences were gradually seen, and their principles and rules noted, and laid down. And in this progress, a natural philosophy was gradually evolved, from the great universal laws of things. And upon the truth of this philosophy, they found that they could implicitly depend, even to mathematical certainty. Therefore, in due time, they raised the mighty telescope, and looked in among the rolling worlds; and learned their comparative magnitudes, distances and revolutions; an event far more astounding in that day, than the steam engine and electric telegraph are in this. For the delusion was then broken. The earth ceased to be the great centre, the main body of the universe; and the sun, moon and stars, mere torches and tapers passing round it to light it. Thus men saw the sizes of our sun and earth, and perceived that the earth was not the primary, but a secondary body, and entirely dependent upon the sun for heat, light, germination and growth; and was daily turning to that sun for blessings, and revolving around him for seasons. And they saw in these things fixed and eternal laws.

With this sure, scientific light in the mind, men now look at the narrative of the creation, and they marvel at the idea, that this little earth, but a mere atom of dust in the balance against the rest, and even cold and opaque in its nature, should have been the first thing created in the whole universe: and that, here it was for a long time, solitary and alone, in boundless space, without sun, moon, or stars, to cheer the gloom; and yet, wonderful to tell, bearing trees and vegetables, contrary to all known laws. And well may man wonder that the enormous sun, the great centre and physical source of a huge system of worlds, should have been the last heavenly body made; or at least, not made until after one of his planets had been three immeasurable days in existence; and bearing trees; days which are now considered, by Biblical scholars, to mean indefinite periods of time; probably not less than a thousand years each; thus leaving the earth alone. in the gloom of its solitude, for thousands of years.

The geologist, also, begins to doubt and demur, as he reads this history of the creation. For, in the process of the earth's formations, he beholds the animal kingdom treading upon the very heels of the vegetable, and mingling with it, at every step of its progressive creation. And he asks how it is possible, that all the animals and fishes, and reptiles and insects, were created on the fifth and sixth days, and all the vegetables and trees on the third, when geology tells so very different a story? For she says the first vegetables were very small mosses upon the rocks, produced after the atmosphere and other elements had prepared the surface of the granite with mould enough to give growth to minute vegetables. And in these little vegetables, before the larger growths were produced, are found, minute animal organizations. And, as we turn over the leaves of the stone book, we see a regular progression of larger vegetables and larger animals, from the smallest up to the production of large animals and trees. This must have taken a long time, so that many animals, besides the creeping things, must have been formed before the earth produced large trees.

Thus the astronomer and geologist are giving up the divinity of the Word. They say, Which shall we believe, God's word or His works? We cannot believe them both, and retain our reason. To this question, the natural philosopher—the strong-minded man, answers, saying, Take His works: believe them; they cannot lie. While the zealous theologian, blindly devoted to the letter of the Word, says, Take the Bible, and let science go: they cannot be reconciled. But a third voice speaks, saying, Take them both: they are God's own books, and they tell the same truths. Read them together, in the light of analogy: each is a key to the other, and verifies its divinity: Read, I beseech you, and every doubt will flee away. The strong-minded philosopher hears this third voice and turns to look. And as the light of correspondences beams into his mind, he beholds the truth of the Holy Word shining through the symbolic language; and he yields the palm, saying, *Both are true.* The astronomer and geologist too, turn to look: and as they see the light of correspondences shining through nature's page in the speech of the written Word, they exclaim, Give God the glory: both books are true. And even the zealous theologian, at last, with caution, turns to look. He reads, and ponders upon correspondences; looks, and hesitates, and looks again, and turns the page backward and forth; but he cannot leave it till he finally cries out, Amen: thy will O God be done: both books are true: Nature and Revelation have met together: Science and Theology have kissed each other.

Let us then look at the sacred history, for that divine light, that we too may see its harmony and beauty and be blessed by its spirit. And in doing this, let us bear in mind, that it is the *soul* of man, that God everywhere speaks about, both in His Word and in His works: that the soul—the mind—is the man; the body is its mere clothing: that this history of the creation has nothing to do with the formation of man's natural body, nor the creation of the natural universe. God had, previous to this history, brought mankind into existence, in numbers we know not how many. They were not yet in the image and likeness of God; because they knew nothing of His love and wisdom. They were simple, ignorant, harmless children of Nature; with no knowledge of soul, mind, God or heaven: distinguished from the brutes only by a capacity to become spiritual. And in this ignorance they would have remained if their heavenly Father had not taught them spiritual things. The Bible, therefore, commences with an account of the process of the elevation of these human souls from natural to spiritual, and of thus making them real men, by giving them the image and likeness of God—the Infinite Man. And the narrative is perfectly applicable now to every person who knows not spiritual things, but applies to the Holy Word for light and becomes regenerated.

The first chapter of Genesis is a complete illustration of the spiritual creation or regeneration of man. It describes, fully and clearly, the order and progress of the regenerate life; or of the creation of the kingdom of heaven or the church in man. And because all things in the macrocosm or material universe correspond to principles in the microcosm or mind of man, they are, in the wisdom of Jehovah, brought up, in this chapter, in such order as to teach most distinctly and precisely, how man may be born again, or raised from natural to spiritual, and thus become a new creature in Jesus Christ. The six days of labor or creation, signify the several distinct states of mind through which we progressively pass from natural to spiritual. The seventh day denotes the spiritual rest we enjoy, when the victory over the evils of our nature is won—when the work is all accomplished—the race triumphantly run, and the warfare ended. It is the Lord that is said to rest: and so it is, for it is He that conquers; it is He that "worketh in us to will and to do."

The internal sense of the Word, of which we shall speak, contains infinitely more than we shall attempt to explain; it being the speech of the Lord, and containing an infinity of principles and relations. Yet, in a partial and modified sense—a sense in which it is at first most receivable by the understanding, it will signify those principles of the mind and that spiritual creation of man which we shall attribute to it. And as we are lecturing expressly for novitiate minds as to the law of analogy, we shall introduce, for explanation, these correspondences which can be most readily seen and acknowledged.

By the creation of the heaven and the earth, in the first verse, is meant the regeneration of the internal and external minds, or the establishment of the church in the soul. "The kingdom of God is within you," says the Lord. By the earth is meant the external mind or the natural and earthly man; and by the heavens the internal mind, or the spiritual and heavenly man. And as the internals of things are always contained within the externals, therefore, when the word "earth" is used alone, in the Word, it means the church or the whole mind, either in order or in disorder, according to the sense in which it is used.

By the earth being "without form, and void," as mentioned in the second verse, is meant, that the mind of man, at the first beginnings of its spiritual creation, is without spiritual truth or goodness. Truth is the form of goodness. To be without form is to have no truth: and to be void is to have no goodness of man's own. This is the state of every unregenerate person. The "face of the deep" is the dark abyss of the obscure and confused state of the mind, without spiritual goodness and truth. The "face of the waters," upon which the Spirit of God moved, are certain hidden principles or germs in man, treasured there by the Lord, called in the Word "remains," upon which the Spirit of God first moves to bring a person to some faint knowledge of goodness and truth It is the implanted conscience ground which a child gets through its good instructions.

"Let there be light and there was light" means, that man began to see that goodness and truth are from the Lord. The light was called "good," because it was good to man to have it. To divide the light from the darkness, was for man to distinguish between the things which were from God and those that were from man's wisdom. For all truth is from the Lord. God called the light day, because it was from himself, giving man a new state of mind. He called the darkness night, because it was man's dark state in the absence of light. The evening and the morning are called the first day, because the evening means the state of shade in the mind, which precedes the reception of some truth; and the morning the state of light which follows. This is what is meant throughout the whole chapter by "evening and morning."

"And God said, Let there be a firmament in the midst of the waters, and let it divide the waters from the waters. And God made the firmament, and divided the waters which were under the firmament from the waters which were above the firmament." How totally dark is this passage in the literal sense! The natural firmament is the sky—the whole immense space in which the stars are placed. Where would the waters be which were above or below this firmament? No human mind can imagine what such language means, without the spiritual sense. But if the waters mean truths, and the firmament the rational plane of the external mind—the heaven of the natural man—then it is easy to see that the waters above the firmament are truths in the natural will, which is above the rational; waters below the firmament are truths in the natural understanding below the rational. And for the Lord to divide the waters which were above the firmament from the waters which were under the firmament would be, to enable man to distinguish between the truths which he loved and those which he only saw; or between truths in the will and those only in the understanding. God called the firmament heaven, because it was the rational sphere of the kingdom which He was establishing in man. This is the second day or a new state of the mind.

"And God said, Let the waters under the heaven be gathered together unto one place, and let the dry land appear. And God called the dry land earth; and the gathering together of the waters called He seas." By the gathering together of the waters under the heavens, is meant the storing up, in the memory of the external man, all the knowledge received from the Lord during regeneration. The memory is the great reservoir of knowledges. Knowledges denote truths signified by waters. And all that we know is our sea of knowledge. The dry land is the good ground of the external mind—the basis of the kingdom of heaven—and is called the earth of the mind. By the Lord's saying, "Let the earth bring forth grass, the herb yielding seed, and the fruit-tree yielding fruit after his kind, whose seed is in itself," is meant the mental earth, or church in the mind, giving germination and growth to the various seeds of truth which have been sown in the dry land, through the Holy Word. This is the third day, or a more advanced state of mind when the fruits of righteousness are produced in the external mind by simple obedience.

"And God said, Let there be lights in the firmament of heaven, to divide the day from the night; and let them be for signs, and for seasons, and for days and years: and let them be for lights in the firmament of the heaven, to give light upon the earth. And God made two great lights; the greater light to rule the day, and the lesser light to rule the night: He made the stars also. And God set them in the firmament of the heaven, to give light upon the earth." Lights in the firmament of heaven are truths in the internal mind—the heaven of the soul. The sun in the heaven of the soul, from its heat, is pure love; it is love to God and man. This is the heavenly Sun which ever speaks or gives off the light of truth. God is love—the Sun of righteousness. The Wisdom which He speaks is THE TRUTH—the Light of the world. The moon in the mind denotes faith, or the truth of faith. The moon is an opaque body; without the light of the sun it is dark. Man's mind is opaque: without truth from God or from love, it is dark. The moon shines only by the light of the sun. Man's mind shines only by the truth of the Lord. The moon, then, is a beautiful symbol of faith. The stars signify fixed principles of truth, or true knowledges in the mind. To set them in the firmament of heaven is to fix them in the internal mind. The lights are set there by means of love to God and faith in Him and His Word. Love to God sets the Sun in our heaven. True faith in Him puts the moon there. And the leading truths of the commandments, when loved, become bright and fixed principles or stars in our mental firmament. For these luminous bodies to give light upon our earth, is for them to illumine and guide our external man. The greater light to rule the day, means that the light of love should govern our affections, in every state of goodness. The lesser light to rule the night, means that the truth of faith may sustain and direct us, in the shady states of temptation ; having the stars or knowledges of truth, in the mean time, as fixed principles in our mental heavens. This is the fourth day, or a new state of mind, when we are in love of the truths, and can walk by their light from within.

"And God said, Let the waters bring forth abundantly the moving creature that hath life, and fowl that may fly above the earth in the open firmament of heaven. And God created great whales, and every living creature that moveth, which the waters brought forth abundantly, after their kind : and God saw that it was good." After love and faith and knowledges of the truths are thus, by the mercy and power of the Lord, established in the soul, and are in active operation, warming the heart into life, from a clear view of right and wrong, the regenerating person begins truly to live. And now commences the creation of principles, within him, which have true intellectual life. They are signified by the creepings things and winged fowl and fishes which the waters brought forth abundantly. Creeping things denote all the lower natural principles of the mind; birds, the thoughts; fishes, things scientific. All these belong to the intellectual region of the mind where truth now reigns. Water is said to bring them forth, because truth cleanses, directs, governs and fills them with life from heaven. All our thoughts have new life: all our creeping inclinations are led by the truth to good; and even our fishes, or scientific principles, are regulated by God's Word, and become living things of the mind. By God's blessing them, and saying, "Be fruitful and multiply, and fill the waters in the seas; and let fowl multiply in the earth," we are taught that everything in the intellectual region of the mind, which has life from the Lord, is ever fruitful, multiplying abundantly. This is the fifth day, or a new state of mind, when the truth comes down from our mental heaven warm with life from love to the Lord, filling all the things of the understanding with living emotions.

"And God said, Let the earth bring forth the living creature after his kind, cattle, and creeping thing, and beast of the earth after his kind.' By the earth's bringing forth the living creature, cattle, beast, and creeping thing, is meant, that the external mind is now being animated with heavenly affections. For animals and beasts denote the affections. And living creatures denote good affections; such as love God and the neighbor. And this is a glorious state in the progress of regeneration, when our soul is filled with love and faith and knowledges of the truth, and is bringing forth every living creature—beast, bird, fish, insect—in true order; when the whole soul, from internals to externals, is truly alive; when every principle of the whole man is fruitful and multiplying with new goods and truths, and producing everything in the Microcosm, or human mind, which the Macrocosm and natural world would produce, if all were right.

"And God said, Let us make man in our image, after our likeness: and let them have dominion over the fish of the sea, and over the fowl of the air, and over the cattle, and over all the earth, and over every creeping thing that creepeth upon the earth." Here we are taught that though God has been, all the while, creating man, yet, that he is not really Man, till he has God's image and likeness: and that he does not fully receive and enjoy these qualities, till he has dominion over the fish of the sea, fowl of the air, the earth, and creeping things. This makes him Man because it gives him freedom. The person who cannot govern himself is not free, and therefore is not worthy the name of Man. And as fish denotes scientifics, and sea, knowledges; so, to have dominion over the fish of the sea, is to have such clear and rational views, from spiritual light, of the scientific principles of our general knowledge, as to keep them from falsifying our reasonings, and biasing our judgment, and thus leading us into deceptive views, and a perverted philosophy. And to have dominion over the fowl of the air, is so to govern all our thoughts, by the divine truth, as to keep them from foggy atmospheres, and wild and visionary schemes of salvation, and from thus running into delusive dreams and false doctrines. To have dominion over the cattle, is to control all our affections by the divine love, that they may fall into no states of unkindness, covetousness nor cruelty; but may ever act from the merciful spirit of Jesus. To have dominion over the creeping things of the earth, is to have the full and perfect control over all the lower appetites and desires of the external man, in all their little selfish wants and wayward suggestions. Thus, as men, in God's image and likeness, we are to have dominion over our entire mental earth, or external man; having every thought, feeling and action — every desire and emotion of the will and understanding—governed by the love and wisdom of the Lord; freely and rationally exercised, as though they were our own principles and powers. This is what gives us true rational freedom, and makes us real men, in the divine image and likeness.

"So God created Man in His own image, in the image of God created He him: male and female created He them." Here we have an account of the creation of Man, male and female. Nothing is said of Adam or Eve; nor of any individuals, as to sex. It is Man or mankind—the race—that is created. "Male and female created He them. And God blessed them, and said unto them, Be fruitful and multiply, and replenish the earth, and subdue it: and have dominion over the fish of the sea, and over the fowl of the air, and over every living thing that moveth upon the earth." From this we see that the work of the creation was not yet completed. They had still got to subdue the earth, and gain the dominion over all the principles of their nature. And to accomplish this they must be fruitful, and multiply, and replenish the external mind, and subdue it. It must be brought under the entire control of the internal mind. To effect this, they must plant the new truths from above in the good soil of the heart, and carefully bring forth the fruits, in the life and conversation. They must increase and multiply their affections and thoughts, for God and their neighbors, from the new goods and truths constantly given them: thus their beasts and birds must bring forth after their kind. This is a regular and progressive work. And the male and female elements which must be engaged in this labor, belong to every individual. Thus each individual can bring forth spiritual things, and must therefore be fruitful and multiply in goods and truths, in himself, or herself. The male elements of the mind are things of the understanding; the female elements are things of the will. The union of these principles is spiritual marriage. It is a union of thoughts and feelings; or of the will and the understanding: or, in its essence, it is a union of good in the will with truth in the understanding. By this union, the mind becomes harmonious, strong, and productive. The understanding, in order, gives us God's image: the will, in order, gives us His likeness. But no one can have either this image or this likeness, unless his will and understanding become united. This is because God's will and understanding, or love and wisdom, are never separated, but are one. And to be like Him ours must also be one. This great work, this new creation, not only unites the will and the understanding, but also the internal and external minds, or the heaven and the earth; thereby, as the work progresses, bringing the whole mind into harmony.

"And God said, Behold I have given you every herb bearing seed, which is upon the face of all the earth, and every tree, in the which is the fruit of a tree yielding seed; to you it shall be for meat." Seeds denote truths. And by the command to take every seed-bearing herb and tree for food we are taught, that every new truth, produced from all the varieties of herbs and trees, or from all the heavenly principles that grow from the good soil of the mental earth, must be loved and cherished in the soul. This is the way to be fruitful, and multiply and replenish the earth. None of the seeds of truth which we bear from the trees and herbs of our life must be lost. The plants must be eaten, and the seeds sown. The way to sow them in our heart is to give them to our neighbor. When we affectionately give the truth to our neighbor, for his salvation, it takes root in our own soul.

"And to every beast of the earth, and to every fowl of the air, and to every thing that creepeth upon the earth, wherein there is life, I have given every green herb for meat." This teaches us that we should bring all our good thoughts, affections and desires, to love, cherish and protect every tender germ and young plant of virtue, denoted by the green herb, which springs from the good ground of the soul: for this also is the way to be fruitful and multiply. Everything good which the heart produces is of God's planting, and should be tenderly cherished. To love a thing is to use it for food, or to make it our own.

"And God saw every thing that He had made, and, behold, it was very good." All things were of course good, because God made them. "And the evening and the morning were the sixth day." The sixth day is that auspicious state of mind when all the thoughts feelings and actions—all the principles of the whole mind are mutually working together for good; and progressing toward that seventh day or sabbath of rest, when the heavens and the earth will be finished and all the host of them.

CHAPTER X.

THE FIRST CHAPTER OF GENESIS IN ITS PRACTICAL BEARING UPON THE REGENERATION OF MAN IN ALL AGES.

"So God created man in His own image; in the image of God created He him: male and female created He them. And God blessed them, and said, Be fruitful, and multiply, and replenish the earth and subdue it." (Gen. i. 27, 28.)

MAN is an immortal soul. Man is a living spirit. Man is an everlasting mind. Man is not matter. He lives here for a brief season in a house of clay. But that house is not the man. That house can neither see nor hear, think nor feel, smell nor taste. It is the soul that does all these things through the body. The body is but a mere instrument, by which the soul operates upon natural things. Take the soul out of it, and what can the body do?

When God breathed into man the breath of lives, God pronounced him a living soul, not a material body. Nor did God breathe that breath of lives into a body of clay, but into an immortal mind, a spiritual body. The soul is primary; the body is secondary. The life of the body is from the soul; the life of the soul from

God. What is God's breath, but the spirit of truth and love? And what is the Word of God but that very breath? God speaks it, that He may breathe that spirit into you and me; that we too may become living souls. For if we receive into our souls the breath of truth and love we are alive unto God. But if not, we are dead in sin, though still immortal. The first chapter of Genesis, before us, contains that holy, living breath of God. It is the spirit and life of Jehovah. And it is given to tell you and me how God makes spiritual and living things. It is given to tell us how He makes the spiritual world rather than the natural: how He makes the souls of men, not their natural bodies; and how He brings those souls into His own image and likeness. And in order to tell us how the souls of men are made, God brings up before our natural thought, in His own divine language and way, an apparent history of the creation of natural things, in order that the things of the soul, "the invisible things of God from the creation of the world may be clearly seen, being understood by the things that are made?"

The reason God brings up these natural things, simply to tell how men's souls are created, is, because these natural things all symbolize principles of the soul. And the history is so composed as to show, by correspondences, the process of the soul's spiritual creation or regeneration. These natural things must signify spiritual things, because God, who is a spirit, made them. And they must denote principles in Him that made them, and still fills them with life, and gives them action. And as man was made in the image and likeness of God, so the things of nature must also denote principles in man.

And now, if we can only look clearly through the symbol to the real, we shall receive some of that spiritual instruction and food for our souls, for which this portion of the Word of God is given. For, think you, the imperishable God speaks the words of eternal life to immortal souls, in merely telling them about the creation of the perishable things of time ? It is of more importance to man to know how one soul is created in the image and likeness of God, than how millions of material worlds are made. For the whole universe of matter is but a mere shadow or reflex of the immortal minds of men. Seeing then, that Man is the world in miniature ; and that the universe of things possesses his qualities, and is a broad symbol of his mind, we can readily see that the creation of the human mind could be very accurately described in every principle and quality, and in a regular and successive development, by a history of the creation of natural things : the history being so composed as clearly to set forth, by the law of analogy, the creation of the minds of men, into the divine image.

Now, if men are not ready to believe our premises, let them look at the matter. Let them *assume* the ground that this history of the creation is a history of the creation of the human mind. That the history is given by God to man, by arranging the things of nature in such order, in the history, as to express, by correspondences, the process of the creation of the human mind. I say, Let them assume this ground, and then look at the history as given solely for that purpose; and a slight glimpse at the law of analogy will show them, rationally, that everything which science or reason objects to, in this whole history, is entirely wiped away; and all appears reasonable and consistent. All the great difficulties are now removed which have so much troubled and perplexed the commentators, respecting the six days of creation as being at war with geology: or in regard to the sun's being made on the fourth day, as opposed to astronomical laws; or concerning the garden of Eden; the trees of the garden; the serpent's talking: the forbidden fruit; and the fall, over which there hangs so much dense darkness: or respecting the creation of Eve from a rib of Adam, after the seventh day; when man had been created, male and female, on the sixth day: or concerning the questions, Who was Cain's wife? and who built the city of Enoch? All these strange things, and many others, will be rationally explained, and the whole history, in a spiritual light, will become profitable for doctrine; teaching the way of life, and the true duty of man to God and his neighbor.

But some people say they take God at his word, in the literal sense, and that that is enough for them. Very well, obey and love the commandments till you. hate evil and love good, and your soul is safe.

But there are others at this day who cannot do that Their intellect demands a reason for belief. The Bible, therefore, must speak to every soul for itself. It is a merciful book and suits itself to all states. I cannot speak to you intelligently, upon the literal sense, alone, of this history. It is dark to me. My understanding demands what the letter alone fails to give. But I can say to you, understandingly, that there is a spiritual sense to be seen, by correspondences, through the literal, which is a history of the creation of the human mind, and is reasonable, beautiful and highly instructive : that it is precisely what the rational faculty, in this scientific age demands : that in the early ages of our race, while the thoughts of man flowed along in union with the divine current, men saw it by intuition : that the science of correspondences was once well understood on this earth, but has long since been lost ; but that many great and good minds have, to some extent, believed in it in all ages ; and that thousands are now embracing it.

Hermes, the great Egyptian legislator, priest and philosopher, who, by his excellence, acquired the name of the *Thrice Great*, and who flourished about the time of Moses, says, "This visible world is but a picture of the invisible, wherein are seen, as in a portraiture, counterfeit forms of more real substances, in the invisible fabric." And this was the prevailing belief of the learned ancients. They believed that the material world was a picture of the world of mind. Philo, who flourished A. D. 40, and who lived in the days of the Saviour, says, "The whole law of Moses is like a living creature, whose body is the literal sense, but whose soul, the more hidden meaning, is covered under the sense of the letter."

Augustine, one of the early fathers of the church, says, "In all things that God hath spoken, in His written word, we must seek for a spiritual meaning." Again he says, "As barley is covered with a stiff chaff, so that you come, with difficulty, to the nourishing part, so the Old Testament is clothed with wrappings or tokens; but if you once come to its marrow, it nourishes and satisfies." Origen, another of the early fathers says, "As a mutual affinity exists between things visible and things invisible, earth and heaven, soul and body; so, also, Holy Scripture is made up of visible and invisible parts: first, a kind of body, or letter, which we see with the eyes, next the soul, or sense which is discovered within the letter." Again, Origen says, "They who find fault with the allegorical expositions of Scripture, and maintain that it has no other meaning than that which the texts shows, take away the key of knowledge."

We could fill a volume with quotations like these from the fathers and early Christians. St. Paul says in Galatians, "It is written that Abraham had two sons, one by a bond-maid, and the other by a free woman, which things are an allegory?" Now, why an allegory? It was a literal fact. And you may read the whole history of Abraham through, and you will see no reason why this was an allegory, any more than all the rest; nor is it.

Many of the deeply pious, in all ages, have supposed there must be some deep signification to the Scriptures, which was not seen in the literal sense. Dr. Adam Clarke says, "I appeal to all persons who have ever read the various comments that have been written on the Mosaic account, whether they have ever yet been satisfied? Who was the serpent? Of what kind? In what way did he seduce the first happy pair? These are questions which remain yet to be answered." Thus speaks Dr. Clarke.

The pious Dr. Watts says, "Who can fathom the depth of the mystery of the Trinity, the fall, the resurrection, &c. But may they not be yet understood? Who can say but that the dark cloud which now overshadows this Mosaic history may some day be removed? Who knows but God may raise up some man to expound these mysteries?" And Dr. Watts was right in his suggestion. For the cloud is being removed. The light is now shining. These great and good men needed only the spiritual sense of the Word, and all would have been plain. Dr. Clarke would have then known who was the serpent. And Dr. Watts would have understood the trinity, the fall, and the resurrection. It was no want of talent nor piety nor human learning that these men saw not the spiritual sense. The rock had first to be smitten before the waters would gush forth. The seals of the Word had first to be broken, before its internal sense could be known. No person could know, from any literal definitions of terms, what was signified by the word serpent. He must first be shown that the serpent denotes a principle in the mind of man, and what that principiple is. Had Dr. Clarke seen this he would never have looked out among the four-footed beasts of the earth, to find what tempted Eve.

With these preliminary remarks we will proceed to the explanation of some of the leading features in the first chapter of Genesis. And you will constantly bear in mind, as we proceed, that the natural things mentioned denote things of the mind ; because the whole subject is the creation of the human mind. Not of one mind or two, and at a certain time, but of any mind or number of minds at any time. And remember, also, that a mind, in a scriptural sense, is never considered created till it is in the image and likeness of God : and that the phrase, "in the beginning," is as applicable to one period of time as to another. There is no beginning with God ; but there is a beginning with everything that is created. And so far as the thing created is concerned, the work is done in the beginning. It is, therefore, but a feeble and fragmentary thought that supposes that at a certain time, in the stillness of eternity, there was nothing in existence but God ; and that He then spoke into being the present universe. What ! The mighty God exist from all eternity up to a certain time without doing anything ? He is an Eternal Creator—"the same yesterday, to-day, and forever"—a Creator always. An Infinite and Eternal God, with an infinite and eternal field to operate in, can always have been and forever be creating finite worlds and things, without filling His field or exhausting His store. He is an eternal cause. And there cannot be a cause without an effect. It will not do to suppose that infinite Love, Wisdom and Power ever existed without action, for that position could belong only to finite and passive things.

The chapter under consideration opens by saying, "In the beginning God created the heaven and the earth." Here commences the history of the creation of some human mind or minds: and it is applicable to any person, or persons, of any age of the world, who are beginning an existence in the image and likeness of God. And, for illustration, let an infant of an hour lie, in imagination, before us. That helpless infant is not a man. But it is a mental germ, possessing planes and tendencies for the possible reception and operation of all the elements of the universe of mind. And with proper influx and development, it will become a man and an angel. The mind to be formed and developed from this infant, by proper influx and action, is to be connected with two worlds; the natural and the spiritual. And could we open that little germ of mind and look into its organization, we should find there an external plane of action, for the cultivation and exercise of thoughts and feelings in relation to this earth, or to material and earthly things. And this earthly plane of the mind is what is meant by the earth which God is said to have created in the beginning. There is also far within that earthly plane of the infant mind, a higher plane, for the cultivation and exercise of thoughts and feelings connected with heaven and heavenly things. This higher plane is what is meant by the heaven which God is said to create in the beginning. But this heaven and earth—this immortal mind—is hidden in the infant germ, in mere tendencies and possibilities, just as the tree is concealed in the tendencies and possibilities of the acorn. And this little mental earth or infant mind is now "without form, and void." The mind, at this early age, has no form or expression of truth. It seems to know nothing rationally. Darkness is, literally, upon the face of the mental deep. But gradually the eyes of the little mind begin to notice things: the brain is being developed, and the child learns things from without, through the senses, and stores them up in the external memory. Thus he grows and obtains knowledge. But it is worldly or natural knowledge: and water corresponds to that knowledge. Now this knowledge is the water upon the face of which the Spirit of God is said to move. As the child is taught to admit and respect the truths of this knowledge, as he obtains them, good ground is formed in his will. And it is because of this good ground, or regard for the truth, that the Spirit of God can move upon the face of the waters. For the Spirit of God is the power of the divine love and wisdom. Thus the youth begins to see the use and feel the force of the commandments: and to distinguish between right and wrong, truth and falsity. The truth of the Word operates upon the face of his knowledge, or upon his regard for the truth. If he had no natural knowledge he could not receive the truth of the Word.

Now, God says to this mind, "Let there be light [or truth]: and there was light." The mind begins now to really see, by the light of the Word, what are some of its natural duties of life. And God saw the light of this mind, that it was good for it. And God divided the light from the darkness: or enabled the mind to distinguish between truth and falsity. And God called the light *day*, because truth is clear; and the darkness He called *night*, because falsity is obscure. The man now begins to see that all truth is from the Lord, and that man's own wisdom is folly. "And the evening and the morning was the first day." The evening is the state of shade and doubt which precedes the reception of truth, and the morning is the state of light which follows. Here is the first day, or the first true state, which a man reaches in the proper development of his mind. He begins to see and regard truths from God. This is a state of natural faith in the Lord. It is the first day or first real light which belongs to the mind.

"And God said, Let there be a firmament in the midst of the waters, and let it divide the waters from the waters. . . . . . . And God called the firmament heaven." This firmament is the rational plane of the external mind—the heaven of the natural man. And its dividing the waters from the waters, is simply its distinguishing between the truths that are in the will, or loved, and those which are only of the understanding, or seen. Waters above the firmament are truths in the affections. Those under the firmament are truths only in the thoughts. And it is important to know whether we love the truth or not. And also to see what truths are loved and what are not.

"And the evening and the morning were the second day." The evening here means the state of shade and doubt upon the subject of truths loved, and truths only seen: and the morning is the new light which follows. Here we see the second day, or true state of mind, which man reaches, in the orderly development of his mental abilities. He now understands the difference between truths loved and truths only seen. This is a state of introduction to works of natural charity. For these truths tell us our duty to our neighbor; and the love of them disposes us to do that duty.

"And God said, Let the waters under the heaven be gathered together unto one place, and let the dry land appear." The waters under heaven are all the truths and knowledges of the external mind. And the gathering of them together, under heaven, is the storing of them up in the external memory. Letting the dry land appear is learning to see and understand things of the will: to know the state of the heart. For the dry land is the will of the external man where the seeds of natural truth are sown. God called the dry land *earth*, because it is the will or soil of the external mind or mental earth. He called the gathering together of the waters *seas*, because seas are waters of the natural earth gathered together, as our knowledges are gathered together in the memory. "And God said, Let the earth bring forth grass, the herb yielding seed, and the fruit tree yielding fruit after his kind, whose seed is in itself, upon the earth." Here the earth, or will of the external mind, is producing or bringing forth good things, peaceful words, and kind actions, as the fruits of the seeds of truth which the Lord has planted.

"And the evening and the morning were the third day." The evening here is the state of shade and doubt upon the subject of obedience and good works. And the morning is the truth and love which follow. And we never perform works of charity, in obedience to God's law, without receiving light and joy as a reward. Here we have the third day, or third state, which a man reaches in the proper development of his mind. He begins now to bring forth the fruits of charity and faith, in good works. Here are the union and ultimate of faith, charity and good works, in the natural plane of the mind. This brings him into a state in which the internal plane of the mind can be opened and illuminated. He is now a good natural man, prepared, by the literal truth of God's Word, for higher light.

"And God said, Let there be light in the firmament of the heaven, . . . to give light upon the earth." The period has now arrived in man's progress when the internal rational of his mind—the firmament of his spiritual heaven—is opened, so that he can receive into his internal man, something of the divine love, the divine truth and true knowledges, symbolized by the sun, moon and stars. Under this state of things, the church—the kingdom of heaven in the soul—begins to arise, and shine ; for its light has come ; and the glory of the Lord is risen upon it. And this light is in the heaven, or internal mind, to give light upon the earth or external mind. And, from henceforth, the natural mind will always have light from above, to which it can look for direction. The Sun of love, or of Righteousness, will rule the day, or when the mind is in a state receptive of new truths, and is rejoicing in the light of love to God and man. And the Moon of faith will rule the night, or when we are in the shades of apathy and selfhood, in the temptations of the world ; having, at the same time, for support the stars of divine truth, prominent in the commandments, as fixed and eternal principles of knowledge, constantly beaming from the mental heaven. Then, should the Lord, the Sun of Righteousness, seem, for a season to be hid from our view, yet, true faith in Him would sustain us with the assurance that our Lord liveth : just as the moon assures us, when the sun is out of sight, that he still shines. The moon, then, like true faith, is truly the evidence of something not seen.

"And the evening and the morning were the fourth day." The evening here is the state of shade and doubt respecting the internal mind ; and the morning is the state of light which follows the illumination of the heaven. Here we have the fourth day or state of the true development of the mind, when the internal plane becomes opened to the reception of the spiritual sense of the Holy Word, whereby the natural man can be governed by higher and clearer truth, and purer love. Up to this time, or during the first three days, the natural mind or earth, only, has been developed ; and that by natural sciences and natural truths of the Word.

The first day, or state of light, was when the Spirit of God moved upon the face of the waters, or excited the affection of the common knowledge of the mind, to see the literal truth of the commandments, causing light or day to be in the mind from God.

The second day or state was when man began to love the truth, and to distinguish between truth loved, and truth only seen : so that he could then divide the waters or truths which were in the understanding from those in the will.

The third day or state was when he began to do the good works, from the union of this love and this truth; denoted by the earth or natural mind bringing forth grass, and herbs, and trees. Thus, the first three days have relation to the understanding, the will, and the action of the natural mind; or to faith, charity and works.

The first day, is the truth seen and acknowledged; the second, is the truth yielded to and loved; the third, is truth obeyed from love, or through faith and charity. This brings the natural mind, or external man, into outward order, by means of natural faith, charity and works, through the literal truth of the Word. But it does not make him a spiritual man. Yet he never could become a spiritual man, till after he had passed through this process. "First that which is natural, and afterward that which is spiritual."

But the fourth day opens our heaven, or internal mind, to the reception of the glorious light of the internal sense of the Word, symbolized by the sun, moon and stars. This light is to come down from our heaven to our earth, to spiritualize the whole natural mind, filling everything with new light and higher life, making natural truth as spiritual; or turning the water into wine; causing our whole natural mind to act from spiritual influences. This change is what God means when he says, "Behold, I make all things new." And for this purpose, the history continues, "And God said, Let the waters bring forth abundantly the moving creature that hath life, and fowl that may fly above the earth in the open firmament of heaven." Thus the waters, the natural truths of the mind become illuminated and impregnated with spiritual life from the Lord, the spiritual Sun. And the history says they brough forth great whales and every living creature that moveth. That is : they brought forth the great sciences of the spiritual doctrines of the Word, and the science of correspondences. And these are indeed great whales. They are the largest scientifics in the sea, or knowledge of the human mind. And thence the very thoughts become spiritually alive. These thoughts are signified by the birds that fly above the earth in the open firmament of heaven.

"And the evening and the morning were the fifth day." The evening is the state of shade and doubt, which we first have in the natural mind, respecting the spiritual sense of the Word ; and the morning is the state which follows the descent of spiritual light from the heaven of the mind into the natural plane. Here we have the fifth day, or state of development, when the natural mind becomes receptive of spiritual light from the kingdom of heaven within. We now give God the glory for every true thought, and for every scientific and rational principle of our mental earth.

"And God said, Let the earth bring forth the living creature after his kind, cattle, and creeping thing, and beast of the earth after his kind : and it was so." Here by the aid of the sun of love, and the moon of faith, and the stars of knowledge, in the heaven of the mind, the natural man or earth is enabled to bring forth beasts and birds, and creeping things which have life: or all good affections, true thoughts, and kind actions. Before the heavens were opened, when we had not the Sun of Righteousness in our heart, or did not truly love the Lord as spirit and life, our earthly mind brought forth nothing but grass, herbs and trees; or the fruits of natural obedience. But now, it brings forth spiritual things, living affections, and heavenly thoughts, signified by beasts, birds, cattle, and creeping things that have life. This is a glorious state of the church when we are filled with true light and life, with heavenly thoughts and feelings of every variety. As this propitious state is reached in the progress of regeneration, and man is about to be completed as far as the spiritual degree, God continues the history by saying, "Let us make Man in our image, after our likeness." That is: Let us now complete the spiritual work, and bring man more fully up into our image, after our likeness. Let us give him what makes him more fully a man, which is "dominion over the fish of the sea, and over the fowl of the air, and over all the earth, and over every creeping thing that creepeth upon the earth." To have dominion over all these things is simply for man to have the government of himself; to control all his thoughts, feelings, affections, passions, and propensities. In this light only can this Scripture be understood. For what dominion has man over the eagle that flies above the mountain summit; or over the wild beast of the impenetrable forest, or the monsters of the unknown deep? But man was to have dominio, over every living creature. Has he got it?

Can he command the soaring vultures or voracious alligators to come down from their heights and up from their depths and stand submissive at his feet, and they obey him? He may shoot them; or entrap and encage them, but that is no dominion. He may lead them by their appetites, or ensnare them by stratagem; but *dominion* means more than this. He cannot call them out, at the fiat of his will, and march them forth at his command. He has no such dominion. Furthermore, he was to have dominion, not only over these creatures, but also over the earth itself. And what control has he over the earth upon which we stand? It rolls on its axis and pursues its annual round, regardless of the will of man. No: it is his mental earth over which he is to have dominion. He was to possess the government over his external or earthly mind and nature. But in order to do this each human mind is endowed with a will and an understanding which are the male and female elements of that mind. For all dominion, and even action, in any person is from the united power of these elements. The understanding is the male element; and the will, the female. When the will is filled with goodness and the understanding with truth, and they become thereby united, they are prepared to work for a dominion over all the principles of the external mind or earth; and even over the entire earthly mind itself. But this dominion is gained only as the mind, by means of this union, becomes fruitful and multiplies in goods and truths, and thereby replenishes the earth, or external mind, with those new goods and truths, as its evils and falses are removed or subdued. Thus is our mental earth to be subdued and brought under subjection to the Lord in the internal mind.

"And God saw every thing that He had made, and, behold, it was very good." God has, thus far, done a good work. But it is not yet completed. The dominion is not yet gained.

"The evening and the morning were the sixth day." The evening is the state of shade and doubt respecting this dominion and the way of obtaining it; and the morning is the new light which shows us the work before us, and how to pursue it. Man is now in God's image, but not in His likeness. He is a spiritual man. This image is *after* God's likeness. The love of the truth gives us God's image. The love of goodness gives us His likeness.

This likeness is to be gained by being fruitful, and multiplying and replenishing the earth, and subduing it. This work, when accomplished, brings us into the seventh day or state of rest, when we possess both the image and the likeness of God, and are prepared to enjoy with delight, the society of the angels of heaven. To be fruitful, and multiply, and replenish the earth, and subdue it, is to cultivate the affections, the ground of the heart, by a good life; sowing therein all the good seeds or truths of the commandments, subduing all the thorns of error, the nettles of vice, the thistles of deception, and the briers of selfishness; until the mind becomes a garden of Eden, filled with good fruits; a paradise of God, cultivated, subdued and replenished; so that we have the complete control over all the birds, beasts and creeping things of our nature, or over all our thoughts, feelings and actions. Then, the kingdom of heaven will be fully established within us. We shall have come to the full sabbath of rest; and all will be happiness and peace. God will bless us, and all the ends of the earth will praise Him.

CHAPTER XI.

THE SECOND CHAPTER OF GENESIS AND THE MAKING OF THE WOMAN OF THE RIB.

"And the LORD God said, It is not good that the man should be alone; I will make him an help meet for him. And the LORD God caused a deep sleep to fall upon Adam, and he slept; and He took one of his ribs, and closed up the flesh instead thereof; and the rib, which the LORD God had taken from man, made He a woman, and brought her unto the man. And Adam said, This is now bone of my bones, and flesh of my flesh: she shall be called Woman because she was taken out of Man."—(Gen. ii. 18, 21, 22, 23.)

IF we would understand God's Word, we must ever remember that it always treats of things of the mind. That the human mind is its universal theme: that natural things are mentioned, only, because they are symbols of things of the mind: and because, in this life, spiritual things can be described, or seen, only through natural things, by correspondences. And though, from a little reflection, we may see that this must be the case, yet we are so natural and so grovelling that we are apt to lose sight of this great fact and fall into darkness and mystery.

Thus, when we read about Adam and Eve, we are apt to think of their material bodies instead of themselves. We think of the mere tabernacles of clay that they lived in, without letting our thoughts ascend up to the inhabitants of these tabernacles, the real beings themselves. Now, until we get into the habit of looking above the mere gross matter of this earth, for men and women, we shall never understand God's Holy Word. Indeed, it is in consequence of our low natural state of mind that the Word seems clothed in such mystery. For, when it is said that the Lord God took from Adam's side a rib, and made a woman of it, who thinks of anything but matter ? a material woman ? Who thinks of her soul, and her life ? Who thinks of any part of her, as coming from any other source than the rib ? The mind, the affections, the will and understanding ; the very woman herself ; everything that can love, and think, and feel ; all that is noble and immortal is not even dreamed of, or taken into the account. And yet these things were never made of matter.

Even the learned commentators have never looked up above the rib for this woman. They have seemed to think that the whole woman ; all there was of her, was made of the man's rib. They do not mention her soul ; but are content to believe that the woman, the wife of Adam, was made of one of his ribs. I commend them for this modesty, and for their humble reliance upon the letter of God's Word. It is all men can know about it, who see no higher than the literal sense. The commentators have tried to believe that the second chapter of Genesis is somewhat explanatory of the first. But every step in that direction has but increased the darkness. Thus, Scott, in commencing his notes upon the second chapter, says, "The sacred historian, having given a brief account of the orderly production of all things, explains, in this chapter, some particulars, more fully, which would otherwise have interrupted the order of his narrative." Here Mr. Scott admits that we have an account of the creation of man, male and female, in the first chapter of Genesis. But, in the first chapter, it does not mention of what material man was made; nor that he was so much as a living soul. It simply says, "God created man in His own image, in the image of God created He him: male and female created He them; and blessed them; and said, Be fruitful, and multiply, and replenish the earth, and subdue it."

But in the second chapter it says, "The LORD God formed man of the dust of the ground, and breathed into his nostrils the breath of lives; and man became a living soul." But no literal reader of the Word supposes that Eve was made at this time with Adam, and received the breath of lives and became a living soul; for the narrative gives the account of her creation afterward, of the rib; but it gives no account of any *breath of lives* being breathed into her, to make her a living soul. Hence the commentators, generally, have taken it for granted, that Eve, the wife of Adam, was made of his rib: and that Adam was made of the dust of the earth.

But the discrepancies between the two chapters are so great, that all attempts to make the second explanatory of the first, have failed. The first chapter says that man—male and female—was made on the sixth day: and we should suppose that they were both made at the same time, and not until after the animals were made. But the second chapter says that Adam, or Man, was first made, and that afterward God planted a garden, and there He put the man; and that He next caused to grow out of the ground, every tree that is pleasant to the sight and good for food; and the tree of life also, in the midst of the garden, and the tree of knowledge of good and evil. Here the man was alone all the time that the trees were growing up, from the planting until they bore fruit. And the man, it seems, in this solitude, with no human being to enjoy these blessings with him, was commanded not to eat of a certain tree. And it seems that he did not eat of it until some time after the command was given, nor until the woman had been made of the rib. For it was not until after Adam had lived in the garden, to see these trees grow up, and bear fruit, and had received the command not to eat of the tree of knowledge of good and evil, and after the Lord God had seen that it was not good for man to be alone, and had promised to make an help meet for him; and also after he had further gone to work and formed every beast of the field, and every fowl of the air, and had brought them to Adam to see what he would call them, and after Adam had given the names to all cattle, and the fowl of the air, and every beast of the field—it was not until after all this had taken place that Eve was formed of the rib, and the forbidden fruit was eaten. Thus, in the first chapter, every other thing was created before man. He was the last thing formed. Man was made male and female on the sixth day. And God said to him, Behold I have given you every herb bearing seed, which is upon the face of the earth, and every tree in the which is the fruit yielding seed : to you it shall be for meat.

But, in the second chapter, it appears that Adam without Eve, was made before the trees were, of which he was to eat ; and before the beasts and birds were made : and that he was put alone in the garden, which God had planted, before the trees had come up : and that the beasts, and birds, and trees, were made after Adam was made, but before Eve was made : and that the command, not to eat of the forbidden fruit was not given to Eve, personally ; but only to Adam : for Eve was not made until some time after the command was given. Now these are all strange things, if we look only to the literal sense. Every attempt to reconcile, or explain them, has only deepened the darkness. And the pious commentator has felt his own weakness in the matter ; and has humbly believed in the mystery, saying, "Let God be true, and every man a liar."

But we should know that all this divine history is about the minds of men, rather than their bodies. It teaches the order of the creation and development of the human mind. It is the immortal soul—the mind—that is the man. It is this that God talks about and cares for. The *spiritual* world—the *eternal* world—the world of mind—is the world which God speaks of creating. Now, if we can only see and acknowledge, that there are two worlds—a world of mind and a world of matter—and that the world of mind has as many things in it as the world of matter has ; and that the things of both worlds are called by the same names, we shall then be able to understand more clearly the teachings of the Holy Word. For we shall see that the mind has its mountains of sin or holiness, its rivers of truth or falsehood, its stars of light, its sun of righteousness, its trees of knowledge, its lambs of innocence, its wolves of cruelty, its foxes of deceit, its serpents of subtlety. We shall indeed see that all the things of nature denote things of the mind. For mind produced them : mind gives them life ; and therefore they must represent the mental quality which gives them form and use. And, as the various principles of the mind bear the same names as the things of nature do which denote them, so we may always readily know something about what God means, when He talks about the things of nature.

Now the Divine Word commences by giving a history of the creation of the human mind ; no matter what natural thing is mentioned, it means something of the mind. And it continues to describe the states and qualities of the human mind until it comes to its close in the Apocalypse. Primarily, it treats of nothing else but the mind. All its creations and falls, its lights and shades, its days and nights, its heats and colds, its times and seasons, its floods and droughts, its clouds and sunshines, its storms and calms, its earthquakes and tempests, its lives, deaths and diseases, wars and tumults ; everything it says describes states and qualities of the minds of men. Yet we are not to lose sight of the fact that there is much literal history in the divine Word, which took place, in this world, as there recorded. But it is, at the same time, a history of the human mind, and accurately describes, by correspondences, the things that were going on there. But there are also many portions of the Word which are given solely on account of the spiritual sense, when the literal events did not occur, as recorded.

Such are the first eleven chapters of Genesis, much of the books of Ezekiel and of the Apocalypse ; and occasional sentences throughout the entire Word ; thrown in to complete the spiritual sense, when the literal event could not occur. This is done because the spiritual sense is the main sense. It is the sense which reaches the soul, and becomes the spiritual and eternal life of them that receive it. And it is not generally difficult to decide whether the literal event occurred or not. For, in all cases, where the literal event is not in harmony with the natural laws, it did not occur.

All the natural laws are laws of God. *Them*, God never acts against. For He cannot act against Himself.

But let us not be hasty to decide against the occurrence of any natural event recorded in the Word. It is the spiritual sense which we can understand which most concerns us. Let us thankfully receive and obey this ; and when further advanced in spiritual life we may be able to see more clearly how far the natural events actually took place.

With these general remarks, let us now glance at the subject of our text, in its spiritual light. For, in this light, all the apparent discrepancies, between the first and second chapters of Genesis, pass away. Remember, it is the *mind* of man that is treated of. And that when the first chapter ends, the mind of man is not finished. It has then only reached a certain state in its progress. There is no such thing as completing or finishing the creation of the human mind. It may progress for ever, and still be incomplete. There will be more knowledge to add to it. It is nothing else than an organized substance of affections and thoughts ; or things of the will and understanding arranged in a human form, in a spiritual body and capable of being taught of God. And such as is the quality of its knowledge and desires, such will be its beauty or deformity, its happiness or misery : and it is free to learn and practise either good or evil.

The word "Man," in the first chapter of Genesis, means mankind—the human race—male and female, without regard to numbers. The history is a history of the creation of the human mind, in mass ; of humanity, or human nature at large. Adam means mankind. The words "Adam and Eve," in their distinct differences, do not mean one man and one woman ; they mean the two great elements of the human mind—the male and female elements ; extending through the whole human family. They mean the Adam or male principle, and the Eve or female principle of the race. These two elements of the mind are the understanding and the will. The understanding, in the spiritual degree of the mind,* is the male principle or

* In the celestial degree, the will is the male and the understanding the female. But in these lectures we explain only to the spiritual sense.

Adam of the mind; and the will is the female principle or Eve of the mind. These principles belong to all minds, both of men and women. Every person, therefore, has his Adam and his Eve of the mind; or his understanding and his will. In the women, the will principle, the love or affections—the female element—predominates. In men, the understanding—the reasoning element—the male principle predominates. And as woman has the broader will, affections, tenderness and mercy; and man the deeper understanding, judgment, reason and courage; so the two brought together make one mind, more full and perfect than either could be by itself. For each supplies the other's deficiency. Their marriage, therefore, gives them that fulness of happiness, which they could not otherwise enjoy.

Now, in order to give, in the first chapter of Genesis, a history of the creation of the human mind in mass, God has apparently given a history of the creation of natural things, because they represent things of the mind. And the things are so arranged, in the history, in their order, as to show the regular creation and development of the mind.

In the order of creation the natural or external man, called the earth of the mind, is always first developed. This development is described in the first chapter by the earth bringing forth grass, and plants, and trees; things which denote principles of the natural mind. Then, as the human race grows up to years of understanding, there follows an account of the creation or development of the internal mind, or heavens, which is described by the creation of the sun, moon and stars, and of the animals ; things which denote the principles of the spiritual mind. Then follows what is called the creation of man, where God says, Let us make man in our image. He had been making man all the while, but had not brought him into His image. This was done by bringing the internal and external minds—their wills and understandings—together, into harmony ; so that the male and female elements of the mind, could work together.

Here closes the first chapter. The mind of the race is becoming spiritual. But their work is not done. The command to them is to be fruitful, and multiply, and replenish the earth, and subdue it ; which shows that the mind, the mental earth, is not yet subdued and replenished. And it also shows that the various principles, which God is giving it, must bring forth after their kind. The race has only now entered upon the sixth day or state. It has not reached the seventh. It has not come to its rest. It has much labor to do first. It is now in its spiritual working state. In this state truth rules.

In the second chapter man progresses on to the celestial state ; or to where love predominates. But this state he does not reach until he has gained the entire control over all the lower principles of his mind, which require much cultivation and development. Therefore, in order to reach this state, God commands him, in the first chapter, to have dominion over the fish of the sea, the fowl of the air, and every living thing that moveth upon the earth. Which means that he shall get control over all the passions, principles and propensities of the mind and body. This would prepare the race for the seventh state of mind, or sabbath of rest, mentioned in the second chapter. For here the Lord says, that, on the seventh day God ended His work which he had made; and He rested on the seventh day from all His work which He had made. This closes the spiritual labor and introduces to a still higher order of things; or to a further development, in which man is to be made celestial, or to be advanced to a state in which love predominates. And, in speaking of this higher state, it is said, in the second chapter, *there was not a man to till the ground.*

Now what does this mean when the whole human race had been created, and had advanced to the spiritual state; and had replenished the earth and subdued it? We shall see what it means by noticing the peculiarity of the terms used in the two chapters, to denote the external plane of the mind. In the first chapter it is called the earth; and in the second chapter it is called the ground. In the first chapter they were to *subdue the earth.* In the second chapter they were to *till the ground.* Subduing the earth is spiritual labor; tilling the ground is celestial labor. Subduing the earth makes it good ground for tilling. The reason there was no man to till the ground is, there was then no celestial man. Man had advanced only to the spiritual state. There were many men to subdue the earth; or to overcome and strengthen the natural mind. But there was not a man to till the ground, or to fill the natural mind with celestial life, by tilling it from love.

The *earth* means the external mind made spiritual, or acting from the love of truth. The *ground* means the external mind made celestial, or acting from the love of good. To replenish the earth, and subdue it is to dispose the external man to do right, because he *sees* it to be right. This is the spiritual state, when the truth rules. To till the ground is to dispose the external man to do right, because he *feels* it to be right. This is the celestial state, when love rules. Therefore it is, that there was said to be no man to till the ground—nobody yet celestial.

You will notice that in the first chapter the *ground* is not mentioned ; but it is the earth that brings forth : and the word *God* only is used. By which we are to understand that the human mind was all the while under the control of the truth, and becoming spiritual, being educated and instructed by truth. But, in advancing man to a higher state, in the second chapter, the word ground is used, and it is the *Lord God* who does the work : or, in the original, Jehovah God, or Love and Truth. In the first chapter it is God, operating as the Truth, that makes man spiritual. But in the second chapter it is Jehovah God, or, both the Truth and Love operating together in the heart, that makes man celestial. Therefore, though it may be thought, by some, that the second chapter is a repetition of man's creation in the first chapter, yet it is not so.

The second chapter takes man where the first leaves him, and advances him on from the spiritual state to the celestial state. And this advancement is described in the following language: "And the LORD God formed man of the dust of the ground, and breathed into his nostrils the breath of lives; and man became a living soul." Here we see that the celestial state is effected by bringing love and good will down into the lowest, smallest things of the external mind—into the very dust of the ground. Now this is accomplished by doing all the little things of life kindly, from the love of the neighbor. Dust denotes the lowest external natural things of man. This work is what forms man of the dust of the ground. It makes him manly in small things. Thus man tills the ground of the mind until the very lowest natural things are filled with celestial love—love to God, and good will toward men. Then the whole man is celestial—lovely. This makes man a living soul; because it makes all his natural affections alive with love

Now he is prepared to make a garden of the mind; because he can now till the ground. Therefore, it is next said that, "the LORD God planted a garden eastward in Eden." This garden of Eden, is the human mind; not of one person, only; but of all the human family then upon the earth. The race was advancing from spiritual to celestial. The trees of this garden are all the principles of the mind growing from the ground of love. The rivers of the garden are truths flowing from the Lord. Here the human family, in this state of paradise, were commanded to dress and keep this garden of the mind. Here all the principles of the mind were made new, and put on the celestial aspect and quality. The very affections of the soul were new; and the people understood their quality: they could read their own hearts.

This state is described in the following language: "Out of the ground the LORD God formed every beast of the field, and every fowl of the air; and brought them unto Adam to see what he would call them." Beasts of the field denote man's affections; and birds of the air, his thoughts. And Adam gave names to them. To name a thing is to ascertain its quality. Thus the human race, at that age, understood the quality of all their affections and thoughts: or, they could give names to all their beasts and birds.

Here, in the second chapter, we see that the animals and trees are created over again. It is because, in the first chapter, these principles of the mind were created from the *truth*: and the *earth* produced them. Now they are created from *love*: and the *ground* gives them forth, and man becomes a living soul. Here we have the highest state to which the human race advanced before the fall; and yet Eve is not mentioned. Here they were, in their purity and happiness. There were many of them, no doubt, in number, both males and females. For we have every reason to believe, that it must have taken many years to advance the human race from a state of entire ignorance, when darkness was upon the face of the deep, up to this high state of celestial light and joy. And how many ages they enjoyed this high state, before they fell, we know not.

But in process of time they found that it was not good to be alone. They wanted a help meet. This uneasy state of mind was the germ of the fall. To be alone is to be single-minded with God. It is to not feel at liberty to act our own way. It is to be one in heart and mind, and one with the Lord. It is to have no two sides to anything; no two parties: but to all yield, implicitly, to the Lord's will, without exercising any independence of thought and feeling contrary to the Lord's will; or following any new inclinations which they might sometimes feel. Thus they gradually began to get tired of this oneness of state, and to want variety; and to think and act more uncontrolled, more in their own way; more as many, than as one alone. They wanted the privilege of saying either yes or no. This state of mind is what is meant by its not being good for man to be alone. It *was* good: but it had ceased to *seem* good to them. Therefore, it is said that, "the Lord God caused a deep sleep to fall upon Adam, and he slept." Adam, here, remember, means the human race, males and females: it means humanity, as it then was, upon the earth. The Lord is said to bring upon mankind this deep sleep, because He is said, in Scripture, to do what He only permits to be done. The human race, in reasoning from their own wisdom and exercising their own proprium, began to fall into a state of darkness and doubt as to whether their wisdom was all from the Lord, or partly from themselves. This darkness and doubt is the *deep sleep*. They were no longer awake and alive to their own duties. Their understandings were becoming dark and their affections cold. The understanding is the male element of the mind, and the will, or heart, is the female element. Thus, the darkened understanding of the race was the Adam that was asleep. And the cold indifferent state of the will was the rib that was taken away. This was done by the Lord by enabling the race to see and understand that men had a selfhood ; and that they were free to exercise that selfhood as their own, and therefore to be no longer alone, provided they would acknowledge that the will, the understanding and the power to do so were of the Lord. This was a new truth that they had not before seen ; and it produced a new state of mind, giving them much joy. For this truth, in the understanding, or in the Adam or male principle of the mind, could be received and warmly embraced by the affections or the Eve principle of the mind. Thus the mind, which was before dark and cold, was now light and warm. This new truth, in the understanding, is the Lord, the Word or the husband. And this new affection of truth in the will is the church, the bride. And this union of good in the will with the truth in the understanding is always used as the symbol of the relation between husband and wife. The race received this new state of the affections, the Eve principle, through the truth in the understanding, which showed them that they were free agents. Thus these affections, or Eve, are said to be taken out of man, because they were received through the truth, in the understanding—the male element : and as the understanding and will are now brought together, it is therefore added that a man shall leave his father and mother and cleave unto his wife, and they twain shall be one flesh. Thus the cold, hard, bony state of the race, was taken away from their affections, or from the side of man, and a warm, soft state, was given in its stead

Bones are often spoken of, in the Word, in reference to the state of the heart, or the affections—the proprium. Thus, the Psalmist says, "Make me to have joy and gladness, that the bones which thou hast broken may rejoice." Here broken bones are broken affections, dejected spirits, or subdued selfhood. Breaking a bone is the same as taking out a rib, or destroying the love of self. Thus it is written, "Hear, O Israel, for my bones are vexed; all my bones are broken; all my bones are out of joint; my bones are consumed." In all these places the self-love or selfhood is meant. Again, "All my bones shall say, Lord, who is like unto Thee?"

Now, one peculiar point of interest, in this subject, and the one of which we should be careful not to lose sight, is the human selfhood or proprium. This selfhood is the mysterious line of distinction between man and his God. It is the point expressive of what there is of man specially; and of what the two different states of man's proprium are—the state in order and the state in disorder: or the state before the rib is taken away and that afterward: for man's selfhood is either dead or alive. It is dead when he loves self for the sake of self. It is alive when he loves self for the sake of the Lord; for then he loves his neighbor as himself. He loves all that God has created, himself among the rest, as the creatures of God's hands, whom God himself loves, and whom we should love also as God's children.

Now, the very point to be noted is this: man had begun to feel some little regard or love for himself, in contradistinction to his love for the Lord. And in trying to study into the nature and quality of his own selfhood and exclusive powers, he fell into that state of profound darkness and doubt, called deep sleep, in which most men are, at this day, upon this very subject of human selfhood. Man, then, wanted to feel himself to be something distinct from his God, and to love himself in this distinction, and to love his God also. He wanted to divide his affections between himself and his God, so as not to be alone, or in oneness in the action of those affections. So the Lord provided that he might love himself or his own selfhood, on condition that he would remember and acknowledge that all that there was which was good in that selfhood, and worthy of his love, was of the Lord alone.

This was a new view of the subject, by means of new light; and they yielded to it. Thus the human selfhood was vivified. The rib, or the cold and dead idea of man's own goodness, was thereby taken away from his mind. Man now saw that he was not good in, and of, himself; and seeing this, and looking to the Lord, the rib, or dead selfhood, was removed, and God's supreme goodness was acknowledged and took its place. Man was now enabled to see himself as finite and distinct from the Lord, and also to love himself for the goods and truths which were in him from the Lord, and not for his own wisdom and righteousness. Man had now, what we call, a vivified, living or spiritual selfhood. This was called flesh, or goodness, in the place of the rib, or lifeless and cold selfhood, which was taken away. This vivified selfhood is the Eve, the

Bride or the Church, in our will, which the truth in our Adam, or our understanding, is to love and embrace. And it is said of them, "What God hath joined together let no man put asunder."

And here we have the true scripture symbol of the conjugial relation between a man and his wife. It is the same as the relation between the Lord and His Church or Truth and Good: or between love in the proprium of man, and the Lord, as the Divine truth, in the understanding. The world is now in great darkness upon this very subject—the human proprium. It is, indeed, in deep sleep, and can only be aroused as the Lord takes from its side a rib, and makes thereof a woman—a good affection—and brings it to the darkened understanding, and they embrace each other.

And this cold, dead bone is being taken away, and the warm living flesh given in its place, whenever men faithfully resist temptations and keep God's laws, as of themselves, with the acknowledgment that the will, the understanding, and the power to do so are of the Lord alone. Thus no person is regenerated without God's taking from his side, or from his affections, the cold rib of his selfhood and putting in the place thereof, warm and generous love to God and the neighbor; and thus forming a union of goodness and truth in his soul, whereby goodness in his heart is the church wedded to the Lord as the Truth. Thus, as in all sacred scripture, we are here taught the way of salvation.

CHAPTER XII.

THE CORRESPONDENCE OF WATER.

" His voice as the sound of many waters." (Rev. i. 15.)

WE speak this evening upon the spiritual signification of water.

Water constitutes one of the leading features of the Holy Word. This is because it denotes one of the principal elements either of the human or of the Divine Mind. It also constitutes one of the leading features and principal elements of the natural world. It signifies truth. And as water is essential to the production and growth of natural things, so truth is essential to the production and growth of mental things. Water, therefore, in every instance in which it is mentioned in the Holy Word, signifies either truth or falsity. And, by the sense in which it is used, it is at once known which way it is to be understood.

Now, because it signifies truth, it is used as an introduction into the church, by baptism. For it is truth which introduces a person into the church. Truths, in the mind, show us our evils, and teach us how to put them away. And, as we repent of our evils, resist temptations and obey the Lord, through the light and power of the truth, we are cleansed from our evils and filled with goods and truths. Baptism by water denotes this cleansing by the truths. It is, therefore, a beautiful and appropriate ordinance of the church, and stands as the great index, pointing the way to heaven by regeneration. Water performs the same use to the body, in cleansing it, and quenching its thirst, and in nourishing and sustaining it, as the truth does to the soul : for the correspondence is perfect.

The very first expression of the operation of God's Spirit, in the Holy Word, is upon the face of the waters. This is made at the commencement of the Divine Word; or, at the beginning of the spiritual creation of the human mind. "And the Spirit of God moved upon the face of the waters." The face denotes the affections ; and the waters, truths. The first effort of the Spirit, after there is light, is, to incline us to have an affection for that light or truth.

Again, water is expressed, as being connected, not only with the first movings of the Spirit mentioned in the Holy Word, but also in the very last exhortation of the Lord to man, in this divine Book. He there says, "And the Spirit and the bride say, Come. And let him that heareth say, Come. And let him that is athirst come. And whosoever will, let him take the water of life freely."

And not only in the first and the last parts, is water used, but also throughout the whole Word. Wells, and rivers, and streams, and rains, and seas, and floods are, all the way, brought to notice. One who has never examined the Divine Word as to the use made of wells of water ; the finding, digging, moving, and destroying of wells, as a means of spiritual instruction, would be forcibly struck with a view of that feature of the Sacred Scriptures.

In 2 Kings we read that the Moabites cast stones on all the good ground, stopped all the wells, and felled all the good trees. Now, if we turn our thoughts from natural things to spiritual, and lay the scene in our own mind, we shall see at a glance, by correspondence, that the Moabites are evil principles or spirits ; that the stones they cast on all the good ground are hard falsities cast on the ground of the mind ; that the wells, stopped, are the sources of truth from the Word hidden from the mind ; and that the good trees, felled, are all the noble and lofty principles of the soul destroyed. What an impressive lesson the Lord here teaches us ! That evils, indulged, will fill our hearts with falsities, close them against the truths of the Word, and destroy the highest and best principles of the soul.

Again, it is recorded in Genesis, that Hagar was sent away from Abraham's house with her child ; that she left the lad under a shrub to die for the want of water, and sat down to weep ; and that God opened her eyes, and she saw a well of water, and she gave the lad to drink. Now, what eyes did the Lord open ? Was it only the natural eyes ? Hagar was not blind in those eyes. Let us then look into our own minds for the illustration : for the Lord would teach us spiritual things. The instruction is given expressly for the present age. Hagar denotes the female element of the mind or our affections, and the child, a new principle or rule of life from the Lord, which our affections love ; and Abraham represents the Lord. And now, if we let these affections go away from Abraham's, or the heavenly Father's, house with the child or new principle, and not continue to look to the Lord for wisdom to feed it, the child will surely die of thirst, or for the want of the water of life. But if, in our wanderings, we feel its need of truths, and fear its death, and set ourselves down to weep and repent of our waywardness, the Lord will open our understandings to the divine truth, and we shall see a well of water springing up from the Holy Word, and we shall give the child to drink.

Again, between Abraham and Abimelech, king of Gerar, there was a falling out ; because Abraham had digged a well, and Abimelech's servants had taken it away ; that is, had taken the credit of digging it. And Abraham and Abimelech entered into a covenant, which was this : Abraham took seven ewe lambs and said to Abimelech, "These ewe lambs shalt thou take, that they may be witness unto me, that I have digged this well." Now, what can this mean ? Why has our heavenly Father recorded such a narrative ? And why is he now giving it to all the world in all languages ? It must be because it contains food for the souls of men. And if we know that the things here mentioned denote things of the mind, and will look within ourselves for them, we shall then see their use and their beauty. Abraham, who is often called father Abraham, represents the Lord as Divine Good. He denotes a principle of love and mercy in our hearts. While Abimelech, king of Gerar, signifies something of the head—the doctrines of faith: Kings always relate to truths.

Now, the Bible talks about wells of water springing up, in the human soul, unto everlasting life. Such wells are always digged by repentance, faith, and obedience. But in order to have this repentance, faith and obedience genuine, so as to produce the well of living water, father Abraham must be there—love to God and the neighbor must be in the work as its motive power or spring of action. Abraham, the heavenly father principle, or Divine Good, digs the well, through the use of the other principles as means of operation. But after the well has been digged, and we are enjoying and giving forth its precious waters, we may carelessly fall into a cold and dark state of mind. And then, while we are reasoning upon the subject in the selfish light of our own intelligence, we may come to the false conclusion that it was by the scientific principles of our own judgment and faith, that the well was digged; that it was Abimelech's servants, or the subjects of our faith, that digged the well, or gave us the truths and doctrines. Thus the merit is all taken away from Abraham, or from the mercy and goodness of God; and we are falling into a dead state of mind; giving up the true religion of the heart, and resting in the coldness of the head alone. Our heavenly Father sees where we are going, and arouses us to a state of our condition and danger. He calls a meeting of Abraham and Abimelech, or of the heart and the head, that we may reflect, and understand where the truths, or waters, and doctrines of our souls come from : whether from wisdom or from love. And, in this examination, he enables us to see that it is goodness that gives forth the truth ; that Abraham digs the well. And now he institutes a covenant between Abraham and Abimelech, or between goodness and truth in us ; or between our understanding and our will. In this covenant, Abraham gives to Abimelech seven ewe lambs to be kept as a witness that Abraham digged the well. or that goodness brings forth the truth.

Now, why should seven ewe lambs be given as this witness ? How could they be a witness that Abraham digged a natural well ? It is because ewe lambs denote innocence of the affections, and seven denotes purity or holiness. Therefore, for Abimelech to receive from Abraham seven ewe lambs, is, spiritually speaking, for the understanding to become convinced, by the truth, that the Divine Good or Father principle is innocent and holy, and that this Divine Good actually brings forth, in us, the truth of the Word, or digs the well. Thus Abraham, or the goodness of God in the will, is to give to Abimelech, or faith in the understanding, a belief in innocence and purity: this belief will cause a union or covenant between goodness and truth in our souls. And we can readily see that so long as Abimelech, or our faith of the head, understands that all purity and innocence are from Abraham, or the Heavenly Father's goodness, we shall of course believe that all truths and doctrines which cleanse the soul, and bring purity and innocence, must also flow from

God's goodness and mercy—that Abraham truly digs the well, or supplies the water.

Again, the Lord commanded Moses to gather the people together at the well Beer ; and the LORD God gave them water. Then Israel sang this song, " Spring up, O well, answer ye out of it ; the well, the princes digged it, the nobles of the people digged it, by the direction of the Lawgiver, with their staves." Now, in the letter alone, we here see nothing practical. It is the same to us as any other history of past events. But if we know that Moses means the Divine Law, and the well Beer means true doctrines, we can see that the Lord is now commanding us, by Moses, to gather ourselves together, at the well Beer ; or to come to the infinite Well, the great fountain of the heavenly doctrines; and the Lord will there give us water, and we shall sing, with Israel, Spring up, O well, in our souls ; and we shall joyfully answer each other out of this well, speaking the truth from the heart. And if we further know that princes mean high and noble principles of the mind, and staves, the power of truth from goodness, we, too, shall rejoice that the princes digged the well in our souls with their staves. For we shall see that it was by the great truths of the Word, through the power of the Lord from goodness, that our hearts became contrite by repentance, and the well of salvation was opened in our soul. And then, if we look a little deeper into the subject, we shall see, at the starting point, that it is the Father's love, through the princes and the staves, that does the work. Abraham really digs the well. And we give to God the glory.

Again, it is declared, in the Word, that the Philistines stopped up all the wells which Abraham's servants digged. Now, as Abraham denotes goodness, so Abraham's servants are those obedient affections of the soul which love goodness, and love to obey its dictates. Through the exercise of these affections the Lord opens in our hearts the wellsprings of life. Philistines denote false principles of the mind which reason against acts of charity and good works as essential to salvation; which place the entire conditions of pardon and heavenly bliss in external wisdom, in faith in God, in worldly science and knowledge. Wells of salvation are doctrines and truths flowing from the heart. When we love the truths of the Word they become our own; and they are a fountain flowing out from the heart in words of wisdom and acts of kindness. But if we yield to the selfish falsities of the Philistine principles, and rely upon our own faith and knowledge, regardless of the duties of charity, these Philistines will surely stop up the wells of the soul which Abraham's servants have digged. Every good affection and kind desire will become blunted and the streams of mercy and truth will cease to flow.

But it is recorded that Isaac digged again the wells which they had digged in the days of Abraham his father: for the Philistines had stopped them after the death of Abraham. Here we are taught that Abraham, or the good principles of the soul, die as they cease to send forth their streams of truth and love, or as the Philistines or false principles, in us, become predominant and stop the wells: but that, even then they can be opened again. Isaac can open them. "Isaac digged again the wells which the Philistines had stopped." Isaac here signifies spiritual love ; or love to the Lord, by means of the spiritual truths of the Word : and how many wells, of doctrine and truth, are now being opened by the love which men feel for the Lord, through the spiritual sense of the Word. This love is the Isaac of the soul, the son of Abraham or of goodness. And if we yield to the spiritual truths of the Word, in humble obedience, Isaac will open, afresh, the well-springs of life ; and we shall heartily bless the Lord at this His second coming, by a life of mercy and truth.

It is recorded that Isaac's servants digged, even in the valley, and found a well. Here we are taught the comforting truth, that, even in the low, selfish hearts or states of men denoted by a valley, when the spiritual sense of the Word comes, convincing the natural understanding of its truth, Isaac's servants, or the affections we form for that truth, by obedience, will open in our hearts a desire to speak the truth, and to love and do it, which is a well. Thus the low, selfish valley will become humble and meek, when Isaac's servants dig the well ; and the water will flow.

Again, it is written that Moses came to Elim where were twelve wells and seventy palm-trees. In the literal sense, we see no essential use to men's souls, by this record. But the spiritual sense is highly beautiful and instructive. The number 12 is the multiple of 3. Three includes everything spiritual—love, wisdom and power. 12 wells signify all the doctrines and truths of the Word. For this reason there were twelve apostles, twelve tribes of Israel, twelve foundations of the Temple, twelve stones in Aaron's breastplate, twelve gates, and twelve angels. Palm-trees denote the spiritual goods of the Word. 70 is the common multiple of 7 and 10. Ten denotes all we have. It is the termination of the man. He has ten fingers and ten toes. We count by tens. Seven is a holy number, denoting purity, fulness and rest. The seventh day signifies a state of holiness and rest. Seventy palm-trees, therefore, denote the holiness and fulness of the spiritual goods of the Word. Places in the Word, always denote states of the mind. Elim denotes a state of mind in the illustration and affection of the Word.

Now, with these significations, we may learn a heavenly lesson, by Moses coming to Elim, where were twelve wells and seventy palm-trees. As all places denote states of mind, so going to a place always means coming into a certain state of mind. Moses means the Divine Law—the truths of the commandments. We are therefore taught by this scripture, that the Divine Law can so come into the soul as to fill it with the illustration, the love, and the enjoyment of all goods and truths. And the practical instruction is this:—If we faithfully and affectionately keep the divine commandments, Moses, or the law of truth and love, will come into the Elim, or the rational plane of our mind, and will fill it with illustration and affection for seeing and enjoying the twelve wells and seventy palm-trees of the Holy Word; or, all the goods and truths which the soul needs or can desire.

Now, we find, in reading the divine narrative, that

there was a great deal of strife and contention among men about wells. Now, why should so much be said about wells? How different is God's history from man's! In God's book, wells are a leading feature: in man's they are never noticed. You may read a whole history of a man or a country now, and not find a well mentioned. It is because wells mean the doctrines and truths of the Word, that they are so often mentioned. It is about truths and doctrines, therefore, and not wells, that the Lord would teach us by these Scriptures.

Now, Isaiah tells us what the true wells of the Holy Word are when he says, "With joy shall they draw water out of the wells of salvation." These wells are hearts which love truth, and love to speak it. The wise man Solomon says, "The words of man's mouth are deep waters"—that "the wellspring of wisdom is a flowing brook." Peter, speaking of persons who had forsaken the right way, says, *They are wells without water.* That is, minds without truth.

Rivers also hold a prominent position in the Holy Word. David says of the good, "They shall drink of the river of thy pleasure." He says, "There is a river, the streams whereof shall make glad the city of our God." That is, the truths of the Word shall make the heart glad in the heavenly doctrines—the Holy City. Again, he says, "The Lord enricheth the earth with the river of God." That is, filleth the mental earth with the truths of the Word.

The Lord showed John *a pure river of water of*

life; which was spiritual truth flowing from God's love.

Moses smote all the rivers of Egypt, and they became blood. All the rivers, ponds and pools, and all the waters in vessels—*all* the water in Egypt became blood! Does any one suppose that this was a literal fact? What certain death it would have been to Moses and all the people to be destitute of water. And how could Moses turn all the water into blood? But in the light of correspondences all is clear. Moses stands for the divine Law which he proclaimed. Blood, which is called the life of the body, denotes, in a good sense, the true life of the soul, or spiritual truth. But, in a bad sense, blood denotes evil life, or falsity, which is the death of the soul. Egypt here means the natural mind; and its rivers and waters, the falsities of that mind.

Now when the truth of the Law falls with power upon these falsities, they are as blood. That is, when the light of the divine commandments shines clearly into the depraved natural mind, its falsities are seen to be carnal life—dead blood. And thus it is that when Moses smites the waters of Egypt they become blood.

Again, it is said of the Lord, "He turneth rivers into a wilderness." Now falsities, which rivers here denote, will make a wilderness of the mind. And God is said to turn them into a wilderness when, by the light of truth, He enables us to see the wilderness state of mind which they have produced.

The Lord says, in Isaiah, "A man shall be as rivers of water in a dry place." A true man is in the image and likeness of his God: and the truth will go forth from him to refresh the thirsty minds around him, like rivers of water in a dry place.

Again, it is said, through Isaiah, "The glorious LORD will be unto us a place of broad rivers and streams; for the LORD is our Lawgiver." Yes, because He is our Lawgiver He will, when we admit Him into our hearts, become in us a place of broad rivers and streams. For His law will be there, sending forth its streams of truth to the world around us.

The Lord says, through Ezekiel, He will bring a sword upon the rivers and destroy their high places. Here the sword is the divine truth. The Lord brings it upon the rivers of falsehood: and He destroys thereby the high places in our mind; or our love of falsities.

The Lord again says, in Ezekiel, He is against the land of Egypt, and against her rivers. By the land of Egypt is here meant the evils of the external man; and, by her rivers, his falsities. And the Lord is always against evils and falsities.

In Ezekiel, the Lord says of Pharoah, "Thou camest forth with thy rivers, and troublest the waters with thy feet, and fouledst their rivers." Pharaoh had become a bad man. His rivers of knowledge had become fouled with falsities. His feet, or lowest natural principles, troubled the waters of truth. It is said that the deep set him up on high with her rivers. That is, he was proud of his knowledge.

In Joel, it is said, "The beasts of the field cry unto the Lord, for the rivers of water are dried up. What do the beasts of the field know of the Lord? It is the

10

affections of men mourning over the want of truth in the world. And well they may mourn, for how sadly are the rivers of water dried up in the hearts of men!

Again, it is written in Joel, that the rivers of Judah shall flow with waters, and a fountain shall come forth of the house of the Lord: where Judah means the church, and her rivers, the truths of the Word.

Again, "The Lord rebuketh the sea, and maketh it dry, and dryeth up the rivers." This, we all know, the Lord does not do, naturally. But He does rebuke and make dry the sea of men's false knowledge, and dries up the rivers of their deceit, whenever they yield to His spirit.

Now, in the passages I have cited from the Word, the necessity of a spiritual sense is readily seen. And so in those I am about to quote, and which I have not time to explain, you will see that there must be a spiritual sense: and many of you will understand it.

"When the poor and needy seek water, and there is none, I the LORD will hear them: I will open rivers in high places, and fountains in the midst of the valleys: I will make the wilderness a pool of water, and the dry land springs of water." Again, "I will pour water upon him that is thirsty, and floods upon the dry ground: I will pour my spirit upon thy seed, and my blessing upon thine offspring." The Lord says of the church, "I entered into covenant with thee, and thou becamest mine, and I washed thee with water, and anointed thee with oil"—or cleansed thee with truth, and filled thee with love.

Again, He says of the church, "I will sprinkle clean

water upon thee, and thou shall be clean from all thine idols." "Except a man be born of water and of the spirit, he cannot enter into the kingdom of God." "The serpent cast out of his mouth water as a flood after the woman."

That waters sometimes mean falses, we might know from what David says, when he prays, "Send thine hand from above ; rid me, and deliver me out of great waters, from the hand of strange children, whose mouth speaketh vanity, and their right hand is a right hand of falsehood." Thus David says, "Save me, O Lord, for the waters have come into my soul. I am come into deep waters where floods overflow me. Let not the floods overflow me, neither let the deep swallow me up." Isaiah says, "I have digged and drunk water ; and with the sole of my feet have I dried up all the rivers of besieged places.

But we need not pursue the investigation further. It must be obvious to all that there is a spiritual signification to water. And that when used in a good sense it means truth ; and in a bad sense falsity. We have mentioned but few of the many passages where water is used.

There is much said, in the Word, of the sea, which means general knowledge stored up in the memory. It may be true, or false, or mixed. In Jeremiah, the Lord says of the church, "I will dry up her sea." Now, what can the sea of the church be, which the Lord can wish to dry up, but her false knowledge ? John says of the coming of the New Jerusalem, "And I saw a new heaven and a new earth : for the first heaven and the first earth were passed away; and there was no more sea." All the false doctrines and knowledges of the natural man, which form the sea of the external memory, are driven away when the spiritual light of the Word enters, creating a new heaven and a new earth. The knowledge now is spiritual. The true water is made wine—the sea is gone. The Lord says, in Mark, " Ye compass sea and land to make one proselyte. Here it is obvious that by sea and land is meant the whole mind of man—knowledge and will.

How beautifully true and expressive, then, is our text! "His voice as the sound of many waters." His voice is divine truth; all truths, everywhere, spiritual and natural: the truths of His Word: the truths of His works: truths of infinite varieties. He speaks in everything. His voice is everywhere. Every truth spoken by man is God's voice. Think of the universal speech of God, wherever the truth is uttered, throughout the vast universe, in all its infinite varieties; it is God's voice. Indeed, *His voice is as the sound of many waters.* May we all learn to hear this voice, so that we can feel the precious presence of our heavenly Father, wherever we are: in city or country: in mountain or valley: in sunshine or storm: on sea or land — whether contemplating His Word or His Works; may the still small voice of His Holy Spirit have our first affections and thoughts, now and forever; for " His voice [is] as the sound of many waters." " And whosoever will, let him take the water of life freely."

CHAPTER XIII.

THE MOSAIC DELUGE.

"And he sent forth a dove from him, to see if the waters were abated from off the face of the ground; but the dove found no rest for the sole of her foot, and she returned unto him into the ark, for the waters were on the face of the whole earth." (Gen. viii. 8, 9.)

WE have seen, by our lectures, that man was the crowning object of the creation, being the connecting link between the earth and the Creator; and containing within him the sum total of the various qualities of the living things of the earth—they being, individually, but component parts of their common lord and sovereign—the human race. We have also seen that man is really and truly man only by means of the church within him; or, in other words, by means of the order and harmony of the various parts and principles of his nature.

From these facts, we have seen that the creation of man, as a spiritual being, is described in allegory, in the first chapter of Genesis, by a composed history of the supposed creation of the world, including the animals and birds, and other living things. And so, by the same law of analogy, the destruction of man, as a spiritual being, in the image and likeness of his God, may be analogically described by a composed history of the supposed destruction of these living things by a flood. And, again, the reëstablishment of this order and life may also be described by a composed narrative of supposed events, in which the living creatures of the earth are represented as brought together into an ark, and there fed and protected against destruction by a flood. And by thus looking at this history of the deluge, in the light of correspondence, as applied to the human mind and its principles, all is rational, beautiful and instructive.

But in trying to view it, literally, as a natural history, it is strange, incomprehensible and at variance with the natural laws. It is incomprehensible because it appears contradictory, unreasonable and inexplicable in itself. In the first place it declares that it rained "40 days and 40 nights," and that the "flood was 40 days upon the earth;" which is a plain indication that the deluge then ceased to prevail. It next avers that the waters continued to rise for 150 days, which is 110 days after it had done raining, and longer than it is affirmed that the flood was upon the earth. We are next told, that, at the end of 150 days, the ark rested on Ararat. This resting of the ark, being just at the time when the water had done rising, would show that the water rose just high enough to set the ark upon the mountain and no more. And, from this time, we are told that the waters returned from off the earth continually; and yet, that it was not until 73 days after the ark had rested, that the tops of the mountains were seen. This would not only make Ararat the highest mountain of the earth, but even so much higher than the rest that the waters had to fall continually for 73 days in order to bring other mountains in sight. We are next told that on the fortieth day, after the tops of the mountains were seen, Noah sent forth a dove to see if the waters had abated. This is certainly a very singular step for Noah to take at this time. Had he forgotten that the ark had been resting on dry land for months, and that the mountains had been in sight for forty days? But, what is more remarkable still, "The dove found no rest for the sole of her foot, for the waters were on the face of the whole earth."

These are strange discrepancies. By the literal sense alone they cannot be reconciled. Nobody has successfully attempted it. The commentators wisely pass them by in silence.

So it appears from the letter, that Noah and his family, with this mass of living creatures, were confined in this ark for one year and ten days. Here they were in this water-tight vessel with only one window, which was but eighteen inches square, and that in the top of the ark—a vessel three stories high, pitched within and without with pitch, with only one door and that closed by the Lord. There is no possible way to account for their existence but by one continued and unaccountable miracle. Such a miracle would be different from all others in the Word; for it is contrary to the laws of life and of order. Such a miracle God never performs: for miracles, when seen by correspondence, are found to be facilities of life in perfect harmony with all the divine laws.

And, by what known law could these creatures have been put into the ark from all the climates and countries of the world: some of them 12,000 miles off, having to pass over oceans, mountains and rivers? I know it is said that God could speak the word and they would be there. But we should remember that God works by means. Why does he not speak the word and make all people good and happy? For "He would have all men to be saved."

The narrative says, "Fifteen cubits upward did the waters prevail, and the mountains were covered." If this is all that the waters rose, the mountains were very low in those days. But the previous verse speaks of the hills being covered: and if this verse means that the waters rose fifteen cubits above the tops of the hills, and the mountains were covered, then the difference between the height of a mountain and that of a hill is only 22½ feet. But it is not to show discrepancies in the letter that we would address you. The letter is all precisely right; all in divine order; there are no contradictions there, when understood. We mention these things to turn your thoughts to something higher, and to assure you that he who puts his trust in the living God, may have his soul rejoiced and strengthened by coming to the spiritual sense; where he will see the Holy Word rising above the cavils of the skeptic and the shafts of infidelity; and commending itself, in every page and verse, to the sober reason with which the wisdom of his God has endowed him.

Let us then, come to that spiritual sense and see what our heavenly Father has for us in this wonderful history : for it is the human mind that is treated of. By the flood is meant falsehoods inundating the mental earth, and destroying its goods and truths ; by the ark is meant, the true doctrines and rules of life from the Holy Word; by the animals, birds and other living creatures brought into the ark are meant the various affections, thoughts and propensities of the mind, brought under the influence of the doctrines of the Word. Thus we may see, by this history, how the kingdom of heaven may be destroyed in man, by indulging in falsities, until every living creature, or good spiritual affection and thought are gone ; and we may also see how we may be raised above all falses and rest upon the mountain of love to God and the neighbor, having every thought and affection restored to order by the rules of life denoted by the ark.

Now, destructions of all spirituality, in the human mind, are often described in the Word by floods of water ; as in the following prophecy of Jeremiah xlvii. 2, " Behold, waters rise up out of the north, and shall be an overflowing flood, and shall overflow the land, and all that is therein ; the city, and them that dwell therein." Here the north, whence the waters come, is a dark and ignorant state of the mind, which gives forth falses : the land which is overflowed, is the will or good ground of the heart : the city which is destroyed, is true doctrines : and they that dwell therein, are all the good principles of the mind. So here we have another flood, of a somewhat similar character to that in Genesis; in which the land is overflowed and the inhabitants destroyed. We all know that this a prophecy of the false state of the Jewish church, and that it has not taken place physically, by inundating their bodies; but that it has occurred spiritually by their falsities.

Again, the Lord says, "Who is this that cometh up as a flood, whose waters are moved as the rivers? Egypt riseth up as a flood, and his waters are moved like the rivers, and he saith, I will go up, and will cover the earth: I will destroy the city and them that dwell therein." (Jer. xlvi. 7, 8.) Here Egypt is the natural mind in its falsities; and another just such a flood is described, covering the earth and destroying the inhabitants. And yet it was all mental; no such flood has ever taken place on the earth.

Again, in Ezekiel, prophesying of the church and its doctrines, the Lord says, "Thus saith the Lord Jehovah, When I shall make thee a desolate city, as the cities that are not inhabited; when I shall bring up the deep upon thee, and great waters shall overflow thee; when I shall bring thee down with them that descend into the pit with the people of olden time." (Ezek. xxvi. 19. 20.) Here is another similar flood; the city denoting the doctrines of the church, and the people the members; the waters, falsehoods. And here the Lord says they shall be destroyed with the people of olden time—alluding to the Mosaic deluge. And as the Jewish church was not destroyed by a physical flood, and yet shared the same fate of the antediluvians, so they must both have been destroyed by mental floods. And so Daniel, when predicting the rejection of Christ and the destruction of the city and sanctuary says, "The end thereof shall be with a flood." The Jews were really immersed in falsehoods and evils. Their spiritual qualities were destroyed by a flood.

And the Lord, in prophetically treating of those who daub with untempered mortar in building the temple of the mind, says, "There shall be an overflowing shower in mine anger, and great hailstones in my fury, to consume it, and I will break down the wall thereof;" which shows that God will suffer the works of all such to be destroyed by a storm of falses of their own creating; for it should be known that God is often said, in Scripture, to do what He only permits to be done. This is the case with regard to all the evils which He is said to bring upon mankind. He is the Creator and Preserver, not a destroyer. Man, by the abuse of his freedom, brings all the evils upon himself. So God is said to cause it to rain and to bring the flood upon the earth. And yet, it is man that brings the flood of falses through the power which God gives him, and which he might use to a better purpose. For by this same power man could look to the Lord, in his freedom, and avoid the curse if he pleased.

The Lord, through Isaiah, speaking of the church, says, "This people refuseth the waters of Shiloah that go softly; therefore, the Lord bringeth up upon them the waters of the river, strong and many, and he shall come up over all his channels, and go over all his banks." (Is. viii. 6, 7.) Here, the waters of Shiloah which go softly, are the gentle truths of the Lord speaking in the still small voice. But when we refuse these kind promptings of the Holy Spirit, we bring upon ourselves the waters of the river, strong and many. Falses, like a torrent, will sweep in upon us, if we refuse to yield to the gentle admonitions of Jesus.

David says, "Save me, O God, for the waters have come into my soul." Now, natural waters cannot touch our souls. Again he says, "I am come into deep waters, where floods overflow me." "Let not the waterfloods overflow me ; neither let the deep swallow me up."

But we need make no more quotations from the Word. It must be obvious that, throughout the Sacred Scriptures, falses destroying spiritual life, are represented by floods of water destroying man. And as waters are used all through the prophets and Psalms to signify truths or falses instead of waters, we must look for the same in Genesis. For there must be a uniform rule for understanding God's language. He being the same yesterday, to-day, and for ever ; so, also, must be His language. And whether He speaks from the book of Nature or that of Revelation : whether in Hebrew or Greek : whether by Moses, the patriarchs, the prophets, the apostles, or John on Patmos, His language is ever and unquestionably the same ; and, like all His works, it is filled with influent principles of spirit and life. And, as the spirit and life of His language is as distinct from the mere letter as cause is from effect, or the sound of man's words from the feelings that utter them, they therefore cannot be clearly seen or appreciated, but by correspondences. But, blessed be the Lord, we are no longer left in darkness or doubt on this subject ; but have a universal rule by which the glorious Word may be opened and explained, from Genesis to Revelation.

One great point to be constantly borne in mind, in the contemplation of the subject of the flood, is, that man is *man* by means of order, or the image of God within him : that the image of God in man, and the church in him, and the love of God and the neighbor, mean the same thing : that when a man loses the image of his Maker, *that* man is said to be dead, or the church in him, consummated : and in this death of the man, the orderly state of his affections and thoughts is destroyed ; which would be described, in divine language, by the destruction of animals and birds. Man is, everywhere in the Word, said to be destroyed by sin—made *dead.* That is, he loses that which makes him truly a man. So were the antediluvians destroyed by sin—swept from the face of the earth, or true pale of the church, by falsehoods.

When man is created anew, or regenerated, all the principles of his thoughts and affections become new, which is represented by the creation of birds and animals, &c. The lion, the lamb, the leopard, the kid, the cow, the bear, the serpent, the dove, the raven, &c., all are new, all in order and harmony. The whole mental earth, the microcosm, with all its teeming inhabitants, is created anew. In this way the lion lies down with the lamb, and the leopard with the kid ; the cow and the bear feed together, and a little child leads them. In this way God enters into covenant with the beasts of the field, and the creeping things of the earth. In this way everything that has breath praises the Lord. In this way the mountains are moved, and the hills skip like young sheep, and the valleys laugh and sing. In this way the church, the kingdom of heaven, is formed by bringing all the animals, birds and creeping things into the ark; or all the principles of the soul into order.

Let us now look at this narrative of the flood, in the light of analogy, and see if we can reconcile its apparent contradictions and impossibilities. The human race was then in a state of great spiritual darkness, brought on by gradually giving up the truths of the understanding to the embrace of the evils of the will.

The events which immediately preceded the flood, and which finally immersed the race in falsities, are declared, in the history, to be these :—"The sons of God saw the daughters of men that they were fair; and they took them wives of all which they chose." This can only be understood spiritually. Truths are the *male* element of the mind, and goods, the *female* element. By sons of God are meant truths in the mind. Every new truth which we receive and love, is really conceived and born in the mind from the word of wisdom sown in the heart. It is *a* son of God. *The* Son of God is all Truth: this Truth is the Christ. And so, by daughters of God are meant goods in the mind. Every good principle we have is a daughter of God, an element of the church, born of God's love in the soul. And had the sons of God taken the daughters of God, all would have been well; for goods and truths are conjugial partners. But they took the daughters of men. By the daughters of men, are meant evils. Whatever comes from man's proprium is not good. God is the only source of good. He only can beget goods in us. He is the heavenly Father of all goods and truths;—of all the children of God. And it is goods and truths, in us, begotten of God, and born in us, that make us His children. This is the new birth. But when the truths of our mind—the sons of God—look upon the evils of our heart—the daughters of men—and think them fair, and come down into their embrace, then the truths become adulterated and falsified by the evils of the will; and thus the whole mental earth may become immersed in falses and errors.

This was the condition of the race, at the time of the flood. The Lord, in mercy, saw their condition, and, in order to save them, instituted a new order of things. For, under every emergency the Lord, in mercy, comes down to men with instructions adapted to their states. By Noah and his family are meant all those who were willing to receive and regard the Lord's instructions. By the ark is meant the church, or the new state of order which the Lord was establishing in their minds as to doctrines and life. The church is now often called the ark of safety. By the materials and dimensions of the ark are meant the character and quality of the doctrines and principles of the church.

This may, at first, strike some as strange and incredible. But this is a rule which holds good, by correspondence throughout the entire Word. Look at the materials and dimensions of the Holy City or New Church doctrines—a city 1,500 miles square, with gates, and walls, and foundations, and precious stones, and gold, and silver, and pearls, and glass, and trees, and rivers, and fruits, all coming down from God, out of heaven, into the human mind. Is the description of the ark, as applied to the principles of the church or the mind, any more strange than this?

By the building of the ark is denoted the practising and establishing, by faithful and humble obedience, these new principles of life in the mind. For these doctrines and rules are various principles of goodness and truth, adapted to the states and wants of that age. And when these principles are received into the mind, that mind is the ark or the church. And though Noah and his family are said to be in the ark, yet the ark is also in them. Men are truly in the church only when the church or kingdom is in them. "I in thee and thou in me," saith the Lord. The three stories of the ark denote the three degrees of the mind—celestial, spiritual and natural. The window in the top, denotes the understanding for the reception of the truth of the Word, the true light of heaven. The door in the side, denotes the reception of the truth by hearing and obeying the commandments of the Word. The window above, denotes also interior or spiritual instruction; and the door below, external or natural instruction. Seeing and hearing are the two most common entries into the mind; and are represented by the window and door of the ark. Noah and his family denote all those who embraced the new doctrines. By their entering the ark is meant their coming under the power and influence of these doctrines and rules of life. By the animals entering the ark is meant the bringing all their various affections within the control of the new, divine rules. The entering of the birds denotes the subjugation of all their thoughts to the divine laws. The clean beasts and cattle denote the good affections of the mind, and the unclean, the bad affections: for, on entering the ark, or coming under the influence of the doctrines, they took with them all their mental principles good and bad. The good are said to go in by sevens, because seven is a holy number denoting purity. And as good affections enter, or as the affections become good, they come into a state of peace and rest signified by *seven.* The bringing of the creeping things into the ark, denotes the control of all the low and grovelling things of the mind by the new divine truths.

But, we are asked, why, if this is a mental ark and flood, is it said to rain forty days and forty nights? This is because the number 40 denotes a full state of temptations. It denotes the whole time that their minds were becoming falsified. Forty is a number often used in the Word for that purpose. Days, or nights, or years denote states of mind: forty days, all the various states of light, and forty nights all the various states or shades of darkness through which we pass during the whole period of our temptations and trials. If we are resisting the temptations and shunning the evils, the states or nights of falsehood and ignorance are disappearing, and all is becoming bright with truth, till we end in eternal day.

But if we are yielding to the temptations, the days or states of light are disappearing ; the Sun of Righteousness is setting ; the moon of faith wanes into darkness ; the stars of true knowledge grow dim and fade away, till the whole mind is inundated with ignorance and falsehood. Forty is a very peculiar number. It is the common multiple of 4 and 10. Ten denotes all we have. It is the termination of the hands and feet. It is the extent of our numbering. We count ten and begin again. Thus we reckon by tens and parts of tens. Four is also a peculiar number. It is the square of two. Two denotes the first two things of all existences—love and wisdom, or goodness and truth. Four denotes the fulness of those principles. That fulness is embraced, by correspondence, in the four cardinal points —East, West, North and South ; in the four seasons of the year—Spring, Summer, Autumn and Winter ; in the four periods of life—infancy, childhood, youth and manhood ; and in the four-square of the Holy City, which includes all the doctrines of the Holy Word. Forty, therefore, is that peculiar number which, by correspondence, denotes the whole process of any thing.

In the book of Numbers, the Lord says, "Ye shall bear your iniquity forty years ; ye shall search the land forty days ;" which means the whole time of their trials and troubles. The Psalms are a full prophecy of the states and trials through which the Lord Himself passed on the earth. And, in them, He says of the Israelites, "Forty years long was I grieved with this generation." Now what does He mean ? He did not live forty years on the earth. He means, by forty years, all the states of His temptations and trials. He assumed the depraved nature of the Israelites, and thus, forty years long He was grieved with this generation; or until He glorified His humanity by putting that generation out of it, and filling it with glory from above. Thus Ezekiel was commanded to lie forty days upon his right side, to bear the iniquity of the house of Judah? Now, why this command? Why lie forty days? Why on the right side? And why would he thus bear the iniquity of the house of Judah? The right side has relation to goodness, the left side to truth. To lie upon the right side is to rest or rely upon the goodness and mercy of God; and forty days would be during all the states and trials of the house of Judah, until their iniquity should pass away.

Hence it is evident why it was ordained, in Deuteronomy, that a wicked man should be beaten with forty stripes: it means that he would receive punishment for all his transgressions: and, why it is said that Moses abode in the mount forty days and forty nights, neither did he eat bread nor drink water, praying for the people: and also why the Lord was tempted in the wilderness forty days; and why the children of Israel were forty years in the wilderness to humble them and to prove them. It is by no means certain that the Israelites were just forty years in the wilderness; or that the Lord was there forty days; or that Moses was praying forty days and nights, on the mount, without eating or drinking: for forty means the whole time, or all the states of trial they passed through.

Let us now look into those strange contradictions of the literal sense, mentioned in this narrative, and see how clearly they are removed by the spiritual sense. In looking back, then, to the time they entered the ark, we behold the people of that age in a state of profound darkness and error: their whole mental earth inundated with falses. In the midst of this general gloom and wretchedness, we see a little band, called Noah and his family, hearkening to the new teachings of the Lord, and forming a little church. They call this church the ark: and they enter into its worship and instructions, bringing under its influence all their wayward and various thoughts, feelings and propensities—every living creature of their mind and heart; and they feed them there with food from heaven, or with divine goods and truths. In this ark or church, they keep their falses under, and thus the ark is raised in their estimation above their own and the surrounding waters of error, until its doctrines rise to the very summit of their affections. They truly love them; the ark rests on the Ararat of their hearts—their love to God and His truth.

And we can now understand how it is that the water could continue to rise so long after it had done raining; and also how it could return from off the earth continually for 113 days, and yet, Noah then send out a dove, and she find the water on the face of the whole earth. It was the earth or mind of the people *in* the ark, upon which the waters or falses thus rose and fell. They entered the ark, or came under the doctrines, with the waters or falses even over their own mountains. Their mental earth was immersed in falses, but they had some life left. And the church or ark was the means by which they were to get rid of those falses and bring their true life into action. They had some remains or germs of life that could be quickened by a righteous life ; and the ark, or new doctrines, was given for this purpose. They were not aware of the depth of their own ignorance and depravity of heart. And it was only as they learned to practise and regard the new truths which were, at first, merely in their understandings, that they could see their falses of heart. For though they had new light in their understanding, adapted to their wants, yet it had not shined upon the mountains of their will. And, therefore, notwithstanding it had done raining, or that they had ceased to receive falses, yet they were ignorant of the extent of their darkness. But as they turned their thoughts inward and explored their hearts from externals to internals, they progressively perceived the various falses of their will. And as they pursued the investigation upwards towards the interior or summit of the heart, they still perceived that, at every new step or day they took, the waters of deceit were there.

Thus the waters are said to rise, after it had done raining, when the rising was all in the perceptions of the people of the church. It was only their increasing ability to see the deeper and still deeper, or higher extent of their falses. The waters were actually there in their hearts, when they entered the ark, or joined the church, but they had not seen them, and the ark had not risen above them. And when, by practising and learning to love the new truths, they had seen and traced the waters of deception up to the very summit of their affections, then it was, and not till then, that the waters could begin to subside from the uppermost pinnacle of the will and let the ark of heavenly truths rest upon the top of the mountain of love and good will. It could not rest there till the waters of deceit were removed. They could not be removed till they were seen. They could be seen, in the more interior states of the heart, only as the people came into higher states of perception. These higher states of the perception of deeper falses are what is meant by the 73 days during which the waters continued to rise after it had done raining, or after they had done practising deceit. And it was not until they had thus obeyed the new truths and truly loved them, or until the ark was on the mountain, that they could effectually put away their evils and falses. And the returning of the waters from off the earth continually, immediately after the ark had rested, was the progressive work of purification of the heart from its falses. Thus it was from off the minds of the church or the people in the ark, and not from those of the world without, that the waters were returning continually till Noah sent forth the dove. And, as they were purified and came into states of true thoughts and feelings, they felt a sincere regard for the salvation of the world of mankind, around them, lying in darkness. And they kindly sent forth the dove to see if the waters or falses were abated from their minds.

The dove corresponds to the Holy Spirit—the spirit of truth and love. This little church then, sent forth that gentle Spirit to the world of mind around, to see if the darkness of error had subsided, and they would accept the truth. But all was still false—dark as night. The dove found no rest for the sole of her foot, for the waters were on the whole face of the earth. No mind could receive the truth. What Christian heart that has a new and heavenly truth, has not experienced the same thing in his efforts to present that truth to other minds ? How often has the gentle dove returned unto him into the ark of his own bosom for a place to rest her foot !

Noah first sent forth a raven—a bird denoting very external truth. This flew to and fro in their external understandings till their falses had so subsided as to receive it. But they could receive nothing higher. It was necessary that they should first have the external truth. "First that which is natural, afterward that which is spiritual."

But Noah, after the return of the dove, waited seven days, or till they had come into new states of mind from the exercise of natural truth: and he sent forth the dove again, or offered them the spirit of truth once more. But their perceptions were still too dark to receive her, and she returned ; and "Lo, in her mouth was an olive-leaf plucked off." The olive-tree, from its oil, denotes celestial love ; the leaf denotes the truth of faith from that love. The return of the dove with the olive-leaf plucked off, denotes that they could receive some little of spiritual truth, or some faith, but could not yet receive the love The leaf was plucked off, or separated from the tree.

Noah waited yet other seven days, or for new states of mind, and sent forth the dove again, and then they received the spirit of truth. Thus the church began to spread among other minds. Now, I am aware that there are many things in this narrative which I have not mentioned ; and about which you are ready to ask questions. But remember that there is matter here for many sermons. I could glance only at the leading features. And I can only add that all may be rationally understood through the science of correspondences : that it is a beautiful, clear and comprehensive description of the fall and regeneration of man. "Forever, O Lord, thy Word is settled in heaven. The righteousness of thy testimonies is everlasting : give me understanding and I shall live."

CHAPTER XIV.

CAIN, ABEL AND SETH ; CAIN'S WIFE AND THE CITY OF ENOCH.

" And Cain knew his wife; and she conceived, and bare Enoch: and he builded a city, and called the name of the city, after the name of his son, Enoch."—(Gen. iv. 17.)

PERHAPS there is no passage in the Holy Word, which has caused more surprise, or been more fruitful of skepticism and cavil, than that of the text. Commentators have puzzled their brains over it for naught. Volumes have been written upon it to no purpose. The question still remains to be asked, by millions, Where did Cain get his wife? or who was she? And well may the candid searcher after truth ask these questions, if he looks only to this literal history for an answer. For the letter alone clearly and definitely teaches, that the human family, at that time, consisted of Adam and Eve, and their son Cain. There is no account of any more births than Cain and Abel. Who, then, could Cain have married? and who built the city of Enoch? And yet, it appears that Cain was afraid, lest every one that should find him would slay him.

Dr. Adam Clarke thinks that Adam and Eve, at this

time, could have had over a thousand descendants. But it is very strange, if Adam and Eve had been populating the world, that the history should mention the names of no daughters, and of only two sons: and should mention them in such a way as to incline the reader to believe that these two children were all they had then had. For, with all the suggestions of Dr. Clarke and others, Eve still declares that her son Seth, who was not born until after Cain had built his city, was the successor of Abel and, to all appearance, the third child. For she said, at his birth, "God hath appointed me another seed instead of Abel, whom Cain slew."

But why should we talk of these strange things of the letter, when the science of correspondences removes the mystery and opens, to the Biblical scholar, a new field of thought; and either closes the mouth of the skeptic, by rational and irrefutable argument, or opens it afresh with songs of praise and thanksgiving to God, for the glorious truths of His Holy Word. For the letter of the history was given solely for the sake of the spiritual sense: and when it was written it was understood; and men read therein only a history of mental things. But, it may be asked, how so deep and obscure a science as that of correspondences could have been understood, at so early an age of the world? We answer: when this science was first known by man, it did not require labor and study to learn and understand it, as it now does. When the human mind was in the image and likeness of God, it saw things in the light of the divine mind. Its thoughts were in the divine current. The divine goods and truths flowed into it;

and it looked down synthetically from causes to effects ; and it consequently understood analogy. Man saw and acted almost instinctively, as a bird builds its nest, or a bee, its cells. He therefore understood the relation between mind and matter ; but not in his own wisdom. Yet, from his having a selfhood, and being free and rational, it appeared to him as though he saw and acted from his own wisdom and power. Still he was capable of understanding that God was all in all, and he was not obliged to fall. But as he fell into sin, and became natural in his thoughts and feelings, he gradually lost his high position and his spirituality, until he finally became entirely natural and selfish. In this downward process, the law of analogy became a mere matter of the memory, and the correspondences were no longer understood. And then, as the people had lost the true light of that science, and as their memory, without that light, was unstable, the correspondences, as a matter of course, became corrupted, and were gradually lost sight of ; and the science became involved in darkness.

But, for a long time, the wise and learned retained that science. And it was their custom and delight to compose fables and imaginary histories of natural things and events, in consecutive order, for the purpose of describing, by analogy, certain mental progressions and developments, or changes and movements of the thoughts and feelings. In this way, the development of a human mind, in all its various and minute changes, from infancy to old age, could be accurately recorded by composing, from day to day, a history of the production, growth and changes of natural things, carefully adapting the history to the mental facts, by correspondences, as they occurred. The first eleven chapters of Genesis, or to the call of Abram, are of this class of writings. They are pure analogy, in composed history, given by our heavenly Father solely for the sake of the internal sense.

The real history of natural things and events commences with the call of Abram. But this history has also an internal sense the same as the other: and many things are there said solely for the sake of the spiritual sense, and which did not outwardly take place. Biblical critics have generally believed in the literal sense, after the call of Abram: but the history, before that time, has been considered, by some of the wise men of all ages, to contain only a hidden sense, and that the literal meaning was not to be regarded as teaching natural events; but merely a vessel containing divine wisdom within it. Origen says, "Who is so weak as to think that God planted a garden, like a husbandman, and in it a tree of life, to be tasted by corporeal teeth: or that the knowledge of good and evil was to be acquired by eating of another tree? And as to God's walking in the garden and man hiding himself from Him among the trees, no man can doubt that these things are to be taken figuratively and not literally." Thus speaks Origen.

That portion of the Bible before the call of Abram is much older than the rest, and belonged to the purely hieroglyphic age. It was a part of a more ancient Divine Word, to a more ancient people. It was transcribed by Moses, by divine direction, and placed at the beginning of the Divine Word, as the proper introduction, directing us back to the very beginning of the creation of anything and everything; and embracing creation during all time. Thus, in tracing back sacred history, we are lost in hieroglyphics when we reach the call of Abram. The letter is no longer reasonable, nor in harmony with the truths of natural science.

But it is not in sacred history alone, that we are so lost. We are equally lost in following back profane history. What do we know of the world's history during the fabulous and heroic ages ? Cast your eye back before the founding of Rome and you are swallowed up in myths. Go back only 800 years before Christ, and you want an interpreter before you can understand the records of that day. Who were the ancestors of Romulus ? History declares that he was brought up in the woods and fed by a wolf. Is this the origin of the founder of Rome, the mistress of the world ? Were the woods his native place ? And were his companions wolves ? The truth is, profane history is here merged in the fogs of fable and symbol ; and no man of this age can read that history.

If we knew what the historian meant by woods and wolves, we might tell something of the character of the early associates of Romulus. These things are true correspondences. We know that woods denote a wild uncultivated state of the mind, and wolf, something of the affections ; and from the quality and habits of this animal, we might know something of the character of the parents and companions of Romulus, if the knowledge and judgment of the historian were reliable :

but here profane history is swallowed up in mythological mysteries. The science of correspondences had become so perverted and adulterated, at that age, that the true meaning of the writings of that day can never be known; but still that Oriental literature contains much more wisdom than is attributed to it. If the ideas were expressed in pure correspondences, they could now be read by the restored law of analogy. But being clothed in the corruptions of that science, much valuable information must be for ever lost to the world.

Now, to find the truth of the text, and of the subject before us, we must bear in mind that the Holy Word, from beginning to end, in its spiritual sense, is a history of the creation and decline of the church, or, in other words, of order and disorder in the human mind; and that this ancient portion of the Word, down to the call of Abram has only the spiritual sense that can teach wisdom. And therefore, by Adam and Eve, Cain, Abel and Seth, as well as all other things mentioned, are meant only principles of the mind, and not persons and things.

Now, the church is composed of two kinds of things—goods and truths, in great varieties. Goods give us God's likeness, and truths, His image. Thus it is the church in man that gives him God's image. The church is really the man. Without the church there is no man. For then, man is not a man, but a beast. The creation of the church, therefore, is the creation of Man. Adam is the generic name for the whole race, males and females. "In the day that God created Man, in the likeness of God made He him; male and female created He them; and blessed them, and called their name Adam." (Gen. v. 1, 2.) By Adam and Eve, Cain, Abel and Seth, are meant things of the church in the human mind.

And now, to clearly see our subject, we must turn our eyes away from the people to the church; to what is within the people, and look at the history there; considering all the people, as to their quality, the church: the truths of the people, the male element of the church, and the goods, the female element; and that every man and woman possesses both of these elements, for every one has truths and goods. Truths and goods are everywhere treated of in the Word, as male and female. Goodness and truth are the elementary principles of all life from God. They are of infinite varieties, and are consequently adapted to all the various things in nature; and they flow from God into all things according to their qualities. The influx of these two living elements is what gives to all nature the male and female principles.

Truth and good united constitute the church. The truth of the first church may properly be called Adam, and the good of that church may be called Eve, because truth is the male principle and good the female. The Lord is called the husband of the church because He is all Truth. And the truth wedded to goodness in our hearts makes us the bride, because it gives us God's image, or establishes the church in us. Adam, then, means the church, or the world of mankind in order—the whole human family before the fall. In distinction from Eve, Adam, in the spiritual sense, means the truth or head of the church, and Eve the good or heart of the church.

Now the church is often spoken of in the Word as conceiving and bringing forth. The kingdom of heaven is like seed cast into the ground. This ground is the goodness or Eve of the church. And this seed is the truth or Adam of the church. The Lord as the Word, is the husband of the church as to goodness. By Adam is also meant the understanding of the church, and by Eve, the will.

Now the circumstances under which the text was recorded were these: the human family on earth had passed out of the garden, or state of happiness, into disorder. And they found that something must be done to restore harmony and peace among them. To accomplish this object this understanding and this will of the people—this Adam and this Eve of the church—set themselves to work to devise some doctrine or means which they could use for the benefit of the church. They needed some rules of life. And they conceived and brought forth the doctrine of faith, and called its name Cain. Faith was the first begotten of the church. They resolved that they would not forget their God; but would believe on Him and acknowledge his supremacy and laws. But they found that one rule of life was not enough. And they brought forth and established another doctrine which was charity; and they called its name Abel.

Thus, Adam, or the understanding of the church or people, in connection with Eve, or the will of the church, brought forth and established, for the guidance and government of the community, these two fundamental doctrines or rules of life—faith and charity—called Cain and Abel. These rules taught them that they must believe in the Lord and regard His laws; and also love one another and live in peace. In consequence of the fall, these rules had become absolutely necessary for the order and safety of the community. Before the fall they needed no such doctrines or rules. The people, then, were the direct and orderly recipients of God's love and wisdom; and they acted out those principles as by intuition, and yet, as though they were their own. But, after the fall, they had to exercise their reason and judgment. Before the fall, they did what they *felt* to be right. After the fall, they had to do what they *saw* to be right. They had eaten of the forbidden fruit—the tree of knowledge of good and evil. Their eyes or understandings were opened. And they had become wise in their own eyes, proud of their own wisdom. This brought discord. Each wanted to rule. And they were under the necessity of looking to the Lord, by faith, and exercising the laws of charity, in order to make life agreeable. And to accomplish this, the church established these two doctrines. They now had faith in the Lord and charity towards the neighbor. And as long as they regarded these doctrines all went on well, of course. This was the best that the Lord could do for them, under the circumstances.

But, as selfishness increased, some ceased to be satisfied with the life of charity: this was more duty to the neighbor than they were willing to perform. And they gradually reasoned themselves into the belief that faith in God was all the doctrine that it was necessary to exercise. As long as they had charity, they offered the firstlings of the flock, or their best affections to the Lord. But the faith of the head began to reason against the offerings of the heart, and these people said to themselves, It is not necessary to our salvation to love our neighbor : faith in God is far better. We need not give away, any longer, the firstlings of the flock—our best affections—for an offering ; we want them for ourselves. Surely, if we give the fruit of the ground, or true faith in the Lord, that will be all-sufficient. Love to the neighbor cannot save us. Salvation is of God. We can do nothing. If we believe in the Lord, he will save us by that faith. Thus the head reasoned against the heart, and the will and the understanding became separated. A strong contention arose between the judgment and the feelings, or between faith and charity, and eventually, the selfishness of the natural, earthly man overruled the better feelings of the heart, and finally destroyed the love of the neighbor.

Thus Cain, or faith slew his brother Abel or charity. The good affections of the heart were destroyed. Faith alone was the cold and selfish state of a portion of the church. The church was therefore divided into two parties. Thus, the Cainites or faith-alone-people, had their own peculiar views distinct from those who still adhered to the principles of charity. But they were unhappy creatures, as all must be who have no true love for one another. "And the LORD said unto Cain,

Where is Abel thy brother? And he said, I know not: am I my brother's keeper?" Thus, in a reflective moment, the Lord as the truth, entered their minds, and they said to themselves, Where is my love to the neighbor? They saw and felt their coldness; and they answered, I know not where my charity is gone. And they answered truly; for they had ceased to be their brother's keeper. Their love of the neighbor was dead. They felt condemned under the light of this truth. They saw that they were not what they should be. And, as said by the Lord, when they should till the ground, or cultivate the mind, it would not yield its strength; for faith without charity can produce no good fruits. The mental earth cannot be cultivated by truth without goodness. And, in their luminous moments, they saw that they were fugitives and vagabonds in the earth, and they were fearful of becoming entirely destroyed or wretched.

But the light, which thus showed them their condition, did not reach their hearts so as to enkindle benevolence, but only to excite selfish fear. And as the truth had failed to call them back to kindness, the next effort of the Lord was to keep them from falling lower. And He therefore said, "Whosoever slayeth Cain, vengeance shall be taken on him seven-fold." That is, the Lord told them, by the truth in their minds, that if they should destroy their faith in Him, or cease to believe in Him, they would be seven-fold more wretched than they were then. Their faith still gave them some connection with the Lord. There was something living in it. And if they should lose that, then indeed they would fall into the lowest wretchedness. He who disbelieves in a God whom he can love is spiritually or mentally most miserable. He has no hope of future existence or heavenly joys. All he can see before him, when this life ends, is darkness and extinction. And even this life loses its brightness and its true delights. These Cainites therefore settled down in the doctrine of faith alone. They became a portion of the church that differed from the main body. And the Lord set a mark upon them that they might be known and preserved. That mark was faith. The ensign of the church from which they had sprung would be *faith and charity*. Name or mark means quality. Faith was the quality or name of the new sect. That was their mark of distinction. And so long as they should wear that mark—so long as they should have faith—they would have some spiritual life.

But, being without charity, the light of their faith in time grew dim and feeble. Thus it is said that Cain went out from the presence of the Lord and dwelt in the land of Nod. They receded from the light and sunk into a vagabond state. Places denote states of mind. Land of Nod, a vagabond state, or a state destitute of goodness and truth.

The world has been long searching in vain for the garden of Eden, the land of Nod, and the city of Enoch which Cain built. But, why should they have searched this earth for the place where Cain went, when it is declared that he was driven from the face of the earth ? Indeed it could not be found, as a *place*, in the vast universe of mind or matter : for it is said to be "*out from the presence of the Lord.*" And where is not the omnipresent God? "If I ascend up into heaven, Thou art there: if I make my bed in hell, behold, Thou art there." Thus we see that the land of Nod must be a state of mind which does not see and love the Lord.

"And Cain knew his wife, and she conceived, and bare Enoch: and he builded a city, and called the name of the city, after the name of his son, Enoch." Now, who, or what was this wife of Cain? Cain was a portion of the church or was a society of men and women who believed in faith alone. Cain also means the faith or the understanding—the male element of that body. And the female element is the will or love of that body. And as soon as these Cainites had cultivated a real love of the idea of faith alone; when the feelings of the heart had become fully wedded to that sentiment of the head, Cain, of course, had a wife; i. e., the will and the understanding were wedded in that doctrine. And then followed the birth of Enoch. This church of Cain could have offspring as well as the church of Adam. Thus these Cainites, through the union of their wills and understandings, gave birth to a whole system of doctrines of faith alone. Enoch, the child born, means these doctrines. This is known, because city means doctrines, and name, quality: and it is said, they builded a city, and called the name of the city after the name of their son, Enoch. The birth of Enoch, therefore, is the establishment of these doctrines of faith alone. And the building of the city is the arrangement of these doctrines into a system of faith.

And now the history goes on, showing the offspring of Enoch, and his descendents, called Irad, and Mehujael, and Methusael, and Lamech, &c. But these are only new rules and principles of the church which originated in their new system of doctrines. But all these new efforts and inventions did not restore order and peace to that ancient people. The loss of Abel could not be made up by all the devices of the head or faith alone. Where charity, the very soul and life of society, is wanting, there is a vacuum which nothing can fill. And this want was fast pervading the whole Adamic people—all the human race of that age.

Under this state of things, something further must be done. Matters could not go on much longer in this way, and be endurable. Therefore, it is written that "Adam knew his wife again ; and she bare a son, and called his name Seth : for God, *said she*, hath appointed me another seed instead of Abel, whom Cain slew."

Here the general church devised a new doctrine or way, which could supply the place of their lost charity or Abel. This new son, Seth, or truth of doctrine, brought forth by the united wisdom and love of the church, was *Good Works.* This son, Seth, which was given by the Lord, instead of charity, was not charity itself, if it had been it would have been called Abel. But it was given for the purpose of restoring charity to the people, for it was given in Abel's stead. And the divine object was thereby accomplished. For the history says that, to Seth was born a son, and they called his name Enos ; and that *then* began men to call upon the name of the LORD.

Thus Seth or good works brought forth love to God and the neighbor. For to call on the name of the Lord is to receive His quality. And this quality includes mercy and kindness toward all. Thus we see here verified the great truth, taught by our Lord, that, if we would enter into life, we must keep the commandments. The Adamic church could not stand without the doctrine of works as a basis. When they found themselves rapidly falling, they established the doctrines of faith and charity; and supposed these were rules of life enough. But faith and charity cannot stand unless they are ultimated and grounded in works. Unless the works of faith and charity are kindly performed, Faith will surely slay his brother Charity.

We now see why Adam gave names to only three children, Faith, Charity and Works. It is because he was the church; and faith, charity and works embrace everything of the church. They are from the three great fundamental principles—Wisdom, Love and Power. The doctrine of works is the doctrine of charity in action. And if we are not charitable, but have natural faith enough to see that we ought to be so, and will then do the works of charity, we shall become so. We now see the necessity of protecting Cain or Faith after he had slain his brother. For without the natural truth of faith, we could not perform good works, and thus be brought into the love of the neighbor, and thereby obtain charity, and thence true spiritual faith.

The lesson we draw from this history is twofold. First, that, if we cease to give to God the firstlings of our flock, or our best affections, and trust to our own faith, we shall lose our charity, fall into a false and lifeless state of mind, and establish ourselves in false doctrines : or, what is the same thing, we shall slay our brother Abel, remove from the presence of the Lord to the land of Nod, marry a wife and build a city. And from this deplorable condition we can never be removed unless, in the second place, there be born unto us, Seth, or good works, and we return to the presence of our God, in humble obedience to His commandments. Then will brother Abel be restored to our bosom, and his blood will no longer cry unto us from the ground.

CHAPTER XV.

A GLANCE AT GOD, MAN AND NATURE, AND THEIR RELATIVE CONNECTION.

"In the beginning God created the heaven and the earth." (Gen. i. 1.)

WE are now to take a general glance at the whole subject of these lectures—God, Man and Nature, and their relative connection, as seen in the divine language. It is a vast theme. We can only glance slightly over some of its leading features.

The subject necessarily commences with God. He is the Great Centre, the Fountain from which everything else proceeds. But here we must remember that, though we commence with the Most High, yet we do not see the Summit. That holy Source of all being, the infinite Jehovah, as He is in Himself, is beyond the reach of the highest finite conception or imagination. No rational thought can possibly be had of Him, by any man or angel, except as He lets His qualities down to our capacities, by clothing them in finite things. And then they can be seen only by the science of correspondences or law of analogy.

This law is the relation which exists between Him

and His Works, and His Word and man. In them, by correspondences, we look towards Him, and get finite but true thoughts of His qualities. For all His works are finite. He has never made anything infinite; nor can He: for infinity can neither be added to nor created. It is self-existent and all. There can be no more. Yet millions of new finite things can be constantly created from It every moment, for ever, without lessening Its varieties or quantity: and all these things are pointing, by correspondences, to qualities of the Divine Being. We may therefore talk about God, we may use the word "Infinite," but we know not what it means. We cannot grasp the full idea it is intended to convey.

Yet, high and holy as Jehovah is Himself, we can know *of* Him. We can feel from his love, think from His wisdom, and act from His power. We can reason and philosophize upon His qualities and laws, as they are symbolized in the innumerable varieties of the qualities, forms and uses of natural things. But without a knowledge of the science of correspondences and of the Holy Word we cannot thus philosophize. We can draw no rational idea of God's nature and character from looking into the things of nature and the human family on earth, as they appear to any natural mind unacquainted with the true Divine Language or Word. No matter how strong the man's intellect, nor how active and powerful his reasoning faculties, nor how extensive and profound his other education, if he is ignorant of the law of analogy and of the divine Word thereby, he can draw from the world and its inhabitants, with all their mixed and contradictory characters, none but blind and erroneous ideas of the Being who brought them into existence. What, he asks, mean the tempests and convulsions, the blights and mildews of nature ; the raving madness of her animals and wild beasts ; the poisonous venom of her reptiles ; and the deceit, murder and vengeance of her people ? Is this the work of Infinite Wisdom and Goodness ? It cannot be ! Thus he reasons. Indeed, the tendency of the whole scene would be to confound and darken his mind, upon the subject of an infinite Creator, and to lead it down to blind nature, as the self-existent and all in all : thus he would rest in materialism ; and suppose that this life would terminate his own existence.

Fallen man can never know himself without instructions from his God. Therefore God has always provided him with divine laws, for his guidance and improvement, suited to his state. But, in the doctrines of the Holy Word, as for many years popularly taught, there is universally acknowledged to be much mystery. With this want of light, the honest, independent, thinking minds of this reason-asking age, are not satisfied. Therefore they give the Bible up as incomprehensible, and consequently, of doubtful origin and authority. And having nowhere else to go they fall into an honest skepticism. For such minds I have a most profound respect and sympathy : for I know their solicitude and suspense. They would be glad of light ; but it must be a light which answers the demands of their reason and judgment. They can receive nothing else.

That light God is now, in mercy, offering to them, in His Holy Word, through the law of analogy. There they will find, as far as they are able to see it, God's true and loving character; and also man's. All discords will be satisfactorily explained: the origin and nature of evil clearly pointed out; the infinite mercy and goodness of God strongly verified; and, as they progress, God will make darkness light before them and crooked things straight. These things will He do unto them, and will not forsake them.

In commencing with God, in this lecture, we have rightly regarded Him as *one*, the Infinite, the Centre, the Source. But in that oneness, there is nothing in all creation, that fully corresponds to Him. If man had never sinned and nothing had been perverted, and all things in nature were in true order, the whole universe, collectively, would correspond to God, so far as He had manifested His various qualities in the creation of angels, men and things. But even that vast whole would be but a very imperfect symbol of the Lord, because the creation is a continuous work, to go on for ever; and every step presents new principles of the divine nature.

Creeping things, then, are but correspondences of principles in God, or in man. And although the varieties, in God's principles, are infinite, yet they are divided into three distinct classes which relate to the three divine essentials in God—Love, Wisdom and Power. It is therefore to something in these principles that every created thing corresponds, either directly or indirectly. For the two great, primary elements, are

Love and Wisdom. Their action is Power. And as they produce everything, all unperverted things must symbolize something of those elements. The number three, therefore, is a full, perfect, and peculiar number: it has relation to everything, either in the complex or in the particulars.

It will aid us much, in our general glance at the relation between God, man and nature, by correspondence, to understand the number 'Three.' The number 'One' denotes God. He is first. Here is the beginning. And as numbers, with the ancients, signified qualities, so number one necessarily denoted God. This correspondence has never been fully lost. We speak of the first man in town; or the first scholar in the class. But when we turn from individuals to principles, number one denotes *Love.* Love is the first principle in existence. It is the first principle in God; and the first principle in man. It is the vital spring of all thought and action; it is the very life element. The next principle in existence is Wisdom. Wisdom therefore is number 'Two;' or two denotes wisdom in its relation to God. But where now is the one? We readily see that it is involved in the two. As we cannot have two things without having one, so neither can we have true wisdom without having love. The next principle in existence, after love and wisdom, is power. Power, therefore, is number three; or three denotes power in its relation to God. But where now are the one and two? They are of course involved in the three. For we cannot have three without having two and one.

This love, wisdom and power then, are inseparable.

Love without wisdom could not think. Wisdom without love could not feel. And the two without power could not act. Thus a regenerated man is in the image of God. His truth or faith is from God's wisdom ; his goodness or charity is from God's love ; and his use or works, is from God's power. Thus the trine in man corresponds to the trine in God. And this trine extends through every created thing. For no single thing exists without having, within it, something from God's love, wisdom and power. For, as love, wisdom and power are inseparable, so the very life which constantly flows from God into every created thing, must contain all these elements, in some of their infinite varieties. And the love is manifested in the substance ; the wisdom, in the form ; and the power, in the use of the thing.

Thus, God, in His love, wisdom and power, is connected with every single thing in the vast universe. But how ? Through man. The first and highest receptacle of God's love is the human will ; of His wisdom, the human understanding ; and of his power, human action. These divine elements, then, before they can become the life of the material universe, must pass through the minds of angels and men. God is the great centre of all being, sending forth the principles of life in every direction, as the sun sends forth his beams. Around Him, and nearest to Him, are the purest minds ; and the farther a mind is from Him, the less pure it is. All are arranged in regular distances according to their qualities. Through these minds, in orderly succession, the stream of life flows, clothing itself, at every step, with the quality of the mind it is traversing, which adapts it to the state of the next. Thus it comes from God, regularly down through the various beings, celestial, spiritual and natural, till it enters men on earth; they clothe it with the quality of their own will and understanding. This gives to the lower orders of things, man's nature, which makes them correspond to him. Thus there is a regular chain of correspondences, or law of analogy, between higher things and lower; connecting them all together. Break this chain, and all would be lost.

But some men say they do not believe in this influx; that it is something new and visionary. Is it something new and visionary, that the Lord is the true Light that lighteth every man that cometh into the world? that His words are spirit and life? that He "giveth life unto the world"? Is this something new? What are this light and life which God giveth to the world? They are either substance or nothing. If they are not real, spiritual substance that can enter the will or understanding, and thus make us feel and think, they are nothing but vagaries of the imagination: mere empty phantoms. Indeed, a man must know that spiritual life and light are love and wisdom, or goodness and truth, before he can have a rational thought of what they are. And then, as he learns to elevate his thoughts, by correspondences, above gross matter, to spiritual things, he will soon be convinced that this Love and Wisdom are the real Source of all substances, and the very elements of Jehovah.

As this divine love flows into an evil man's will, it has, all the way, in its descent from God, through mediums, been clothed in lower and more impure substances, until the evil spirits associated with the man adapt it to his state. And though the inmost of this influx is pure love or life from God, yet as its power must be acted out through its vile covering, the influence, as it goes forth, will be evil. And as it flows from this selfish, quarrelsome will into the beasts of the earth, it gives poison to the serpent's tooth, and contention to the dogs for their bones. And so of the influx through all other men's minds, according to their various qualities ; some adapting it to the lambs and doves, some to the bears and wolves, and others to all other creatures and things : little children being the medium of life to lambs.

Now, from a little reflection, it may be rationally seen that this living influx from the Divine Mind, must, in substance, be feelings and thoughts. For what else can mind give forth ? And when we, in this life, give true thoughts and good feelings to a willing mind that has not before received them, we know that that mind is sensibly affected by them. Again, we may rationally see that God's thoughts must be principles of truth, and His feelings, principles of goodness ; and that, in order to take effect, these truths must flow into understandings, and these goods into wills ; and that these wills and understandings, which first receive them from the Lord, must be of a very high character, in order to appreciate and use them. Thus it is philosophical and rational to believe that the order of influx is from higher things into lower. And who does not see that every man gives a certain caste or coloring to what passes through his mind. It does not go out as it comes in. He puts his own feelings into it. It partakes of the qualities of the mind it passes through. Thus, let Mr. Webster and Mr. Clay witness the same event ; and as they describe it, it comes from one Websterized, and from the other Clayized.

Now, as man was the sole object of the creation, being the only creature endowed with rationality and freedom, whereby he can distinguish between right and wrong, good and evil, truth and falsity ; and thence be capable of knowing and loving his God, and thereby becoming connected with Him, by His goodness and truth seen and loved, and thus enjoying heavenly happiness and living forever ; so, we may rationally see that this freedom necessarily gave man the power of abusing this liberty and rationality, by an evil life, so that his will and understanding would become selfish and deceitful, and thereby change the character of the Divine Influx, and give to the lower orders of things the evil and quarrelsome propensities of men. Indeed this is the only rational ground of the origin of evil that has ever been suggested. For, upon any other ground, God is the direct Author of it. But, upon this true ground, it sprang from the abuse of those principles, without which man would be a machine, destitute of freedom or reason.

To understand our subject, then, we must never lose sight of the Trine of first principles and their qualities. *That* is the key to all true knowledge of spiritual things. Everything should remind us of it, and point us, by correspondence, to God, in His Love, Wisdom and Power. God is the life of the universe ; the All in all of everything, by means of the trine of essentials, seen by correspondence. It is only in that one great idea, that we can have a rational thought of God. It is only in a true idea of the trine, in its united substance of love and wisdom in action, that we can rationally see God in nature or in man, and know that He dwells there.

By an idea of the trine and its qualities, we, by correspondence, can see God in the sun, the earth, the animal, the tree, the flower ; in anything. To know a thing is to know its qualities. The idea of a thing amounts to nothing, if that idea contains no thought of its qualities : for it then has nothing in it but darkness and ignorance. What does the idea of life amount to if we do not know that it is love, and real substance ? Simply, nothing. For a want of substance is a want of everything. How long the learned world has puzzled itself over the idea of life, and left the subject as dark as they found it, for the want of knowing that it *was something.* But when we think of it as substantial love, we have something tangible in our thought ; something that we can *feel* to be true. And what can we know of thought until we see that it is something either true or false, exercised or moved by that love ? Indeed we see nothing right, unless our thought reaches back to God, and rests in the Fountain—the Great First Cause—by rational correspondence.

Without the great truth that love and wisdom are substance, centred in God and flowing into man, enabling him to feel, think and act, men have supposed that thought and feeling originate in the brain of the material body. And seeing not that life is received substance all has been dark. And when they look at nature, and behold her teeming with life, in all its varieties ; and have no idea of the origin, substance and quality of that life, the same darkness hangs over nature. And when, by the aid of natural science, they geologically search nature for the first manifestations of this life, and find it, in the mineral kingdom, in the most feeble expressions ; it seems to act from the rock as its author. They next see it, in a higher and stronger influence, in the vegetable ; still higher and stronger in the animal ; and highest and strongest of all, in man. But the higher things seem dependent upon the lower for their life and existence ; and all upon the dead cold mineral. Thus nature appears to them as everything—the very mother of all—and to which they of course must return at death. Here all is total darkness. They see not how lower things can produce the higher ; the cold dead mineral giving forth the beautiful vegetable, with its delicate texture and velvet flowers ; and the insensitive vegetable giving forth living creatures with the five senses of animal life ; and man, above all, with his sublime powers of mind, resting upon these inferior things, as his origin.

Alas ! What darkness ! But this is the best that nature can do. Without instruction from God, man could never know anything higher. But with the Holy Word before him, instead of looking down to inert matter, as the source of his being, he can look up to his God. And by a knowledge of Him, in the substance and qualities of the trine, a flood of light, by correspondence, is poured into his mind. He sees the stream of the love, wisdom and power of his God, flowing down through higher things into lower, till it reaches the mineral kingdom, as a ground of reaction; when it returns back to God, in the gratitude, love and praise of human hearts.

This trine of principles, in the light of analogy, is the key of knowledge. All knowledge is of and from God. It is He that breaks the seals and opens the books; and all by this key to His own qualities. From these qualities we are to judge of the qualities of everything, more feebly or more fully expressed in some things than in others; and in either direct or inverted order. Everything charming and lovely in nature has the trine there. All colors are from heat, light and action. The heat denoting God's love; the light, His wisdom; and the action, His power. And those divine essentials are really in the colors. And all their beauty is from the presence of God. Take God's love, wisdom and power out of the sun and it would be dark and powerless. All words are from vowels, consonants and arrangements. The vowels denote love, the consonants, wisdom, and the arrangement, power. Thus God is in our speech in every word we utter. If the speech be false, His principles are perverted. He is also in the feeling, thought and action which speak the word, as well as in the word itself. All music is from tones, sentiments and activities; denoting love, wisdom and power. God therefore is in all music. Every thought of man has its affection, its idea, and its action. The divine elements are there. Every organ of the body or mind has its form, its substance, and its use, and points to God's qualities. Everything in the universe, below man, has in it something from man's love, wisdom and activity ; and, by real substance, corresponds to something in man ; and also to something in God ; either in direct or in inverted order.

The highest symbol of God in any one thing, except the human mind—the highest symbol of Him in nature is the sun ; the heat denoting His love, the light, His wisdom, and their action, His power. And when we consider the sun as corresponding to God, and the earth to man, we have a broad field for contemplation, and one which throws much light upon the understanding of the Holy Word.

Let us glance at the similitude between the earth and the mind. The first general division of the earth is into land and water : that of the mind into will and understanding. The land denotes the good or evil ground of the will, and the water the truth or falsity of the understanding. The land can produce nothing without water : nor can the will without the understanding. Goodness can do nothing without truth, nor evil without falsity. But even the land and water together can produce nothing of themselves alone. They must have the heat and light of the sun. So also must the will and understanding of man have the love and wisdom of God—the divine influx—or they can do nothing. The land and water of the earth denote the will and understanding of the external mind, or the natural good and truth which are in them. To be truly alive and productive in heavenly things, this natural will and understanding must receive spiritual goods and truths from the internal mind. This internal mind is represented by the natural heavens, with the sun, moon and stars. The sun denoting the Lord, the moon, faith in Him, and the stars, knowledges of His commandments.

And how forcibly does the power of these divine principles, from our internal mind, operating upon our external, correspond to the influence of those heavenly bodies, upon the earth, without which it would be utterly unfruitful. Thus the correspondences between the physical universe and the human mind are everywhere, most perfect, not only in generals but in particulars. And it is necessarily so, because the elements of the human mind are the living elements of the universe, by regular influx :—first God, then man, then nature : Man the connecting link between God above him, and Nature below him : Man having two minds —an internal and an external—one connecting him with God and heaven, the other with the earth and nature : Nature the mirror of man, in which he may see reflected, every quality of his soul, to the very life : and God, in His Holy Word, holding that mirror up before our face, in every page, from Genesis to Revelation, showing us thereby, a full-length portrait of humanity in its creation, its fall, and its regeneration. And the particular character of each individual, from infancy to his present moment ; and even his future path which will make him either an angel or an evil spirit, is also clearly delineated. He sees clearly which way to go and what to do ; and *that*, in legible characters, imperishable words, written by the eternal law of analogy. So full and perfect is this delineation, that a man well versed in the science of correspondences and a knowledge of the Word, and filled with the spirit of Jesus, will yet look upon the page of nature, in the light of analogy, and read therein, his soul's history written by his own hand, recorded by his own life, in all its lights and shades, whether good or evil. If he sees two animals fighting, he will know whether it is through his disposition that they are stimulated to quarrel. If he loves to see them fight his own soul is in the combat.

These are the glorious truths which will yet lift the veil from human hearts and minds ; bring the world together in wisdom and love ; break the shackles from every heart ; banish discords from all bosoms ; open every prison door ; loose every captive ; discharge all jailors and hangmen ; do away with courts and juries; make every man a judge and a peace officer, with a jurisdiction extending over all his own life and conduct, submitting himself, with gladness and delight to the divine government, in all those precious golden rules of life, which fill the soul with love to God and good will toward men. Then will the knowledge of the Lord cover the earth, as the waters cover the sea ; tears will be wiped from off all faces; the kingdom of God will be here; and His *Will* will be done on earth as it is done in heaven.

CHAPTER XVI.

THE RESTORATION OF THE SCIENCE OF CORRESPONDENCES.

" Behold, I make all things new." (Rev. xxi. 5.)

Our present theme is the way and manner in which the long lost Science of Correspondences has been restored, and thereby, the spiritual sense of the Word and the life of its doctrines, revealed.

1863 years ago, when our Lord made His appearance in the flesh, human nature was at its lowest state of sin and depravity. To this wretched condition the race had gradually fallen, during thousands of years, from a state of innocence and virtue in the garden of Eden.

In his highest primeval condition, man's mind was in true order. He saw from internals to externals. He saw effects from the causes which produced them. He saw the world of matter as an outbirth from the world of mind. In seeing this, he saw that a perfect analogy existed between material and mental things. He therefore saw the qualities of the thoughts and feelings of God and man perfectly represented in the material forms around him. He saw that material things could not possibly exist but as the effects of will and wisdom from above ; and that, therefore, they must be true manifestations of that will and wisdom.

In all this, he saw the true language ; the divine language ; the hieroglyphic language ; the only universal language ; the first written language ; the only undisguised and certain expression of thoughts and feelings.

But, in this clear preception of things, man had but a mere shade of will and thought of his own. He felt and saw, almost exclusively, from the divine love and wisdom. His mind was but little else than a mere undeveloped vessel, receiving goodness and truth from the Lord, and giving them forth in feelings and thoughts.

Yet he had a selfhood given him, that he might be something more than a mere machine : for, without this selfhood, he would have been incapable of progress and rational enjoyment ; therefore he would not have been a man. The essence of this selfhood was rationality and freedom ; reason to determine, and freedom to act, as a distinct individual.

In consequence of this selfhood, it appeared to man as though the wisdom and love by which he saw and acted were his own ; but he was also capable of understanding that this will and wisdom were not entirely his own, but were principally the Lord's. The truth is, this selfhood gave him a will and understanding *as* his own ; but, in this intuitive condition, this will and understanding were in perfect harmony with the divine love and wisdom, and acted with them. Yet it appeared to man as though he were thinking and acting entirely from his own free-will.

This selfhood, therefore, necessarily made man free to reason and act, either as from his own will and wisdom, or as from the Lord's; and, as it seemed to him that he felt and acted entirely from himself, his selfhood made him capable of using the Lord's love and wisdom as his own, and of falling, by habit, into the selfish belief that they were really his own, and that he was perfectly competent to manage his own affairs himself. Therefore, in the ability to look to the Lord, and progress upwards, was the ability to look to himself, and decline into evil. Man was free to take either course. He took the latter. Hence the long progressive fall, from the primeval age to the coming of the Lord in the flesh.

In this downward process, man lost the divine language, founded on the science of correspondences; and with it he lost all true knowledge of the world of causes, or of the laws of creation, and the relation between mind and matter. He entirely lost his internal standpoint, where he could see in unison with God's wisdom; and he took his position in the dark, sensual depravity of the external mind, where he saw things, not as they really were, but only as they appeared to be. Thus everything in his nature had become perverted. He saw himself as the very centre of all being, and the universe as the circumference; and thus he was about to perish for the want of light and life.

In this state of things, our heavenly Father, that He might restore man again to order and true life, came and took his central position again in our nature. He took upon Himself, by conception and birth, human nature, in the omega, as it then was. He became again the centre, and that humanity, the circumference. Still, that humanity, as assumed, had a will not in harmony with the divine will. It still had its own centre in the circumference of things, and its natural inclination was to look and act from that apparent centre. But, by its connection with the Great Divine Centre, it was enabled gradually to change its position, and to see from the divine will and wisdom.

This was effected by its yielding up its own will to the divine will, in the midst of temptations and trials, until everything in that nature which was impure and ungodly was seen by that nature in the divine light, as not good, and freely rejected, and put away. Thus that nature, by free-will and consent, became perfected and glorified, and made one with the Father; the whole having one will, and that will divine—the very Centre of all existences.

Thus, having conquered and overcome all evil influences in our nature and come near to us in the letter and spirit of the gospel, the Lord was able to reach and draw all men toward Him, who would yield to the influence of the truth of His Word. But men were then so low, sensual, and natural, that they could not receive spiritual truth. They could not be at once elevated into the spiritual light of causes, where they could look down again upon effects, and see them in their true light. They had, therefore, to be reached in the circumference where they were. Here they could be reached only by natural truth and good; and to effect even this, they had to be overawed by the power of the Lord's miracles, and forced into an assent and submission to things which they did not understand. But by their faith in the power of the Lord, and obedience to His commandments, they, by actual experience, gradually saw and felt the truth and goodness arising from righteousness of life, repented of their natural evils, and, in their degree, became regenerated.

Some of the disciples appear to have had, at times, glimpses of higher light ; but they could not retain it, and the simple letter of the Word—the natural truth —was all that they could bear. But it is very certain that some of the most spiritually-minded of the disciples and early fathers of the church were sensible that there must be some higher meaning to the Word than the letter ; but the subject was so new, so high, and so vast, that their natural state could not receive it. The Christian church, therefore, settled down upon the literal sense of the Word, with wholesome doctrines drawn therefrom ; and all who have sincerely received these literal truths, faithfully repented of their sins, and regulated their lives by the commandments, through faith in the Lord, have found their way to happiness and heaven.

But, not being able to receive spiritual truths, this state of things did not last, as the Savior declared that it would not. The dark ages came on. The church declined in doctrines and in life. " The traditions of men made the commandments of God of none effect." Schisms and division ensued, carrying martyrdom, bloodshed, fire, and fagot in their train, until the people were anything else than the followers of the meek and lowly Jesus, loving their enemies, and rendering good for evil.

This crisis was reached about one hundred years ago; and the Lord declares of it in Matt. xxiv. 22, that "except those days should be shortened, there should no flesh be saved." Under this state of things, what could be done? The true nature of God had been lost sight of, and the true way of life. All the doctrines of the Word were falsified. How could man be reached? Nothing short of an entire new light, differing *in toto* from anything the world then had, could elevate the race. They wanted a new God, a new Bible, new doctrines, and new truths, before they could be moved one step upwards. And yet all the needed, new life, and light, and doctrines were in the old Bible before them; but they could not see them.

But, though they had been becoming blind to the true light of the gospel, yet men had been making rapid progress in natural science. Their natural faculties, and powers of reasoning, had become greatly developed; and many were becoming prepared to look for some rational ground of religious faith. Nothing else could now reach their wants. Human nature had grown up to natural manhood. Its intellectual eyes, in the natural plane, were opened; and it was asking for light in matters of religion as well as science. Marvel and mystery could no longer satisfy or control the free mind, and there were some living remnants in fragmentary Israel who were hungering and thirsting for something to satisfy the longing soul. But they knew not what it was, nor where to find it. The period had, therefore, fully come, when something new must be done, and when something new could be done.

There were minds now that could begin to receive the spiritual sense of the Word, if it could only be brought scientifically before them. This sense was the only thing that could lead their thoughts to the true God, give them right views of His nature, and faith in His Holy Word. The lost Science of Correspondences was the only key to that spiritual sense that would fit their minds. If that science could be brought rationally before the minds of men, so as to enable them, from their low, natural position, to look understandingly up through the world of effects to the world of causes—through natural things to spiritual, material to mental, —so as to see and receive spiritual light from the Holy Word, then the human race on earth could be gradually elevated to heavenly order and happiness; otherwise man must perish. "Except these days should be shortened, no flesh should be saved."

By the use, then, of the key of correspondences, the seals of the Word could be broken, and the Book opened. But who was able to do it? None but the "Lion of the tribe of Judah could prevail to open the Book, and loose the seals thereof." The seals were all in the human mind. It was sealed with seven seals; that is, every state of the human mind was closed against spiritual light. Man was altogether natural. But there were some minds in a religious state of natural good, and in such a state of natural-rational freedom as to be able to have their minds opened by instruction from the Lord, so as to see spiritual light through natural symbols, could they be so instructed.

But how was this mighty work to be done? How

was the human mind to be opened and instructed, so as to behold the wonderful things written in God's law; to see the glory of the world of causes, and to look down upon effects, and see them as they really are? There was but one way to do it; and that was for a man to take the Holy Word, give it his supreme time and attention, and work out its wonderful problems step by step; proving every operation, as he went along, by the truths of the Word itself, looking to the Divine Master for instruction. Thus the mind, in this new study, would have to be as gradually opened, enlightened, and expanded, in spiritual science, as minds are naturally in the pursuit of natural science.

But a mind, to do this work, must be a mind in a state of strong natural truth and good. It must be a mind possessing rational and unwavering faith in the Lord, in the divinity of the Word, and in the work before him; a mind humble, prayerful, open, and confiding towards the Lord. But where was the mind to be found competent to the task of going to this Fountain of wisdom, working out its spiritual problems, and spreading out before the world a clear and satisfactory solution of the work, proved and authenticated by the Divine Truth itself?

EMANUEL SWEDENBORG was the man, in the Divine Providence, for this work. But what peculiar qualifications had he for entering upon a study so high and heavenly? From his youth, his training and education had prepared his mind for just such a work. With always a conscientious regard for the Bible, and a love of truth and virtue, he had mastered all the human literature of the age; deeply investigated the laws of matter in the mineral, vegetable, and animal kingdoms; had traced the economy of the human body up to the soul, and nature up to God; and had rationally seen something of the relation between mind and matter, and the laws of creation. In this way, his natural mind had become a sincere and open vessel, adapted to the reception of spiritual truth; and his active soul was thirsting for something higher, and looking up to receive it. And thus, at the mature age of fifty-five years—ripe in natural goodness and truth, and in scientific and literary wisdom—he was prepared to enter upon the divine study of the Holy Word in its spiritual sense.

This study rationally opened his mind to the laws of the spiritual world; so that he gradually came, while in the flesh, into a state of free, open, and sensible consciousness of spiritual society and scenery, and this by a process of such perfect mental growth and development, according to divine order, that, when his spiritual senses had become clearly opened to the spiritual world, they were permanently so; because his views of that world were not surface and uncertain views, presented from a disordered or inflated imagination, but they were scientific views. He saw and understood the law by which spiritual forms are manifested, and this law he found in the Holy Word. It is the SCIENCE OF CORRESPONDENCES, in which the Word is written, and which he labored to make known to the world; and, in the ardent exercise of this benevolent desire to give it freely to his fellow-man, his soul was rationally opened to receive it from the Lord.

Twenty-nine years of intense application were devoted to this work, in which he presented to mankind twenty massive volumes, opening and expounding the Sacred Scriptures, and specifically recording his illustrations, and the Science of Correspondences by which they are explained. This he did in the most modest and quiet manner, without any startling miracles or outward displays of power, but in a deep, calm, and contemplative state of mind; looking prayerfully and confidingly to the Lord while reading the Word.

In this way, the Science of Correspondences, and the spiritual sense of the Word and its doctrines, have been presented to the world. But who has done it? Certainly not Swedenborg, but the Lord Himself. Swedenborg never, in all these volumes, gives us so much as a single opinion of his own upon the meaning of the Word or its doctrines, or of the Science of Correspondences; but the illustrations are so given as to make the Word itself its own interpreter. It is the Lord, therefore, and not Swedenborg, that speaks to the heart and the head of the reader of these volumes. Yet Swedenborg was not inspired. He acted not as an amanuensis, as did the prophets. He freely saw and understood what he wrote. He knew it was true; but he knew, also, that it was not, one particle of it, his own wisdom; and he was far from claiming it.

These twenty volumes, therefore, in their explanations of the Word and its doctrines, become to the understanding reader positive and conclusive evidence of their own truth and the truth of the Holy Word. They call in an array of testimony which carries everything before it. They call our own internal selves and experience on to the stand, with all our evils, and all we know of human nature, and make them cry out, Amen! They call in to their support all the truths of science and art. Indeed, they call in everything,—the vast universe of mind and matter, and the law of analogy between them. Everything in nature, from the smallest dust of the earth to the sun in the heavens, bears testimony in these volumes to the truth of the Word, and the divinity of its Author; proving, beyond a doubt, that the Creator of the universe is the Author of the Holy Word; that the spiritual truths of the Word are the Divine Wisdom by which God created and sustains the universe; and that the universe now stands in relation to that wisdom, as effects to causes. All this is satisfactorily proved by the law of analogy which pervades the whole Word. Man therefore rests in the evidence of these volumes, as God's own testimony of the truth of His Word; for by them the Lord opens the seals of every mind that reads and understands them: and as man turns from his evils, and yields his heart to this light, the Lord gradually purifies and elevates his thoughts and feelings above falsehoods and evils to heavenly light and life.

What a vast work this Science of Correspondences, and the consequent influent spiritual light from the Word, have laid out before them! It is nothing less than the entire revolutionizing of the whole mental world on earth, and the restoring of all things to order,—an entire change of all man's views of God, of man, and of nature; placing man in an entirely new position, where he will see with new eyes and in a new light, and, by obedience, will learn to feel with a new heart.

The starting point in this elevation is a true thought of God—some ray of light from the Great Divine Centre into the rational faculty, presenting some true idea of God's nature and character. In the light of this idea, presented to man's rational consciousness, lies the whole revolutionizing power. As we read the Holy Word in the light of this idea, that light brightens and expands into the Sun of Righteousness, and becomes, indeed, the Jehovah God; and we then see Him to be Love, Wisdom, and Power, in union as a whole. And we see this Love, Wisdom, and Power ever going out from the centre of the universe, creating, sustaining, and giving life to everything. We see in this divine character no change or shadow of turning, but infinite and equal mercy towards all.

In this divine light, the Holy Word presents us with a new Author, and with new doctrines, differing in every particular from those entertained by mankind a hundred years ago. Indeed, then, does the Lord, at His second coming, "make all things new." He makes us see all His own creations and doings to be good, and all evil as springing from man: therefore we see man falling and going astray, and God following him up to save him. But, as we see that man could not fall without the free exercise of his own will and judgment, so also we see that he cannot rise without their free exercise. God gives to man the power to turn from his evil way, and live. This power is in the truth which man sees. The starting-point in this change is the truth so presented to his mind that his own free-will and judgment tell him that the thoughts, feelings and actions in which he is indulging are wrong, and lead to misery and death. The regenerating power that this truth really contains is in the light that it brings of God's true nature, telling us we must be like Him, and that in Him is our only dependence and help. This light the Science of Correspondences everywhere forcibly presents to view in the Holy Word. Hence the regenerating power of the Lord at His second coming.

The Science of Correspondences keeps God's glorious and merciful character before us in every page of the Word, and it shows us what is meant by everything that the literal sense seems to present of Him of a different character. It shows why the Word was so written, and the use; and both senses become thereby perfectly harmonious. Thus we see that the literal truth of the Word flowing into an angry man's mind, presents the merciful God to him as angry: just as the light which falls upon a crooked and imperfect mirror reflects a beautiful face as distorted and ugly. The anger is in the man, as the imperfection is in the glass. The bad man looks at the truth which condemns him, as his enemy; when it is really his friend in effort to save him.

Thus the Lion of the tribe of Judah, according to prophecy, has prevailed to open the Book, and loose the seals of God's Holy Word; and has mercifully given to the world the Divine Science of Correspondénces—the grand key which opens the door to that fountain of wisdom which is to bring the world into order.

These twenty volumes, with the Holy Word which they open, will yet stand before the world as the great test by which the truth or falsehood of every new system, creed, or practice, which may spring up in this fruitful age of wonders, will be tried. All sects and parties will yet come to these volumes, and the Divine Word, for light; and their decision will be peremptory and final: for there will be found nothing substantial upon which to base an argument against them. They will be regarded as the Great Universal Body of Divinity, the true standard of all wisdom, the basis of all law and order. Nothing can supplant them; for they centre everything in God. Nothing can rise above them; for they give to God the highest excellence. No truth can oppose them; for they are the fountain and embodiment of all truth. The doctrines they present are one harmonious whole, with Jesus in the midst. Their tendency is to show man his sins in such a light as to convince him that they are his certain destruction, and then to show him how to get rid of them in a way so plain that he cannot mistake it. This is their universal tendency, and in this great work they must in due time succeed; purifying, regenerating, and making happy, the whole human family on earth. What this due time will be, no one can tell. The race was many thousands of years in falling from the *alpha* of its existence in the Garden of Eden, down to the *omega* of our nature at the divine incarnation. It may take as many thousands of years to bring us up to full millenial life and glory: but the movement must ever be with accelerating force and influence; for its sphere is amid free and active minds, first enlightening the understanding, and then gaining the heart. And all it gains it holds forever. And its final success is certain: for the Lord declares of it, that "God shall wipe away all tears from their eyes; and there shall be no more death, neither sorrow nor crying."—"And there shall be no more saying, every man to his neighbor, Know ye the Lord; for all shall know Him, from the least unto the greatest: for the mouth of Jehovah hath spoken it."

THE END.

www.ingramcontent.com/pod-product-compliance
Lightning Source LLC
LaVergne TN
LVHW010219110826
845151LV00004B/1141

9781425527518